Fisher

February 23, 2009

# CALL AGAINST
# THE WILL

# CALL AGAINST THE WILL

## GOD'S CALL TO A STUBBORN PHONE MAN CREATED MASTER PROVISIONS, A GLOBAL CHRISTIAN CLOTHING MINISTRY

### ROGER BABIK

MASTER Provisions
Walton, KY

CALL AGAINST THE WILL
God's Call to a Stubborn Phone Man Created MASTER
Provisions, a Global Christian Clothing Ministry
by Roger Babik

MASTER Provisions
12236 Hutton Drive
Walton, KY 41094
roger@masterprovisions.org
http://www.masterprovisions.org

ISBN-13: 978-0-9790463-7-7
ISBN-10: 0-9790463-7-8

Library of Congress Control Number: 2006936661

Softcover
First Edition, 2006

Cover and book design: 1106 Design

# Table of Contents

# *Dedication*

A godly wife, willing to invest her life into the precious lives of four children, represents an irreplaceable gift in my life. Tanya Oakes Babik commandeered lots of single-parent days and nights as home school teacher and nurturing mother during the hectic early years of ministry. My humble attempts to simultaneously juggle full-time work at Cincinnati Bell with founding a mission ministry, while serving as a Deacon, Chairman of Missions, coach, husband and father would have floundered had it not been for you. The faith in God you displayed when "Doc" told us cancer's fury gave you six to twelve months left to live inspired many people, especially me. Thanks, honey, for your faithfulness, consistency and bluntness when needed. You're an awesome wife and Lydia, Jerrod, Leah and Joy are blessed children. All of you bless me more than you will ever realize!

Praying parents, Jerry and Susan Babik, laid the foundation for full-time Christian service. From my earliest recollections, they were always faithful in praying that all of the Babik kids would follow Jesus and enjoy a Christian marriage. They were always willing to host missionaries in our home and set an example through liberal giving. Dad's call to heaven came on June 8, 2004, and now I repeat the same words to you that Dad uttered before he drew his final breath: "I love you!"

Tanya, Mom, Dad, Lydia, Jerrod, Leah and Joy: My life's work is to please God and this dedication is a small way to says "thanks" for all of the sacrifices you made on my behalf. I love y'all!

Praise the Lord All the Time!

Roger

# Introduction

What does God want me to do if I grow up?  Now that I'm "all grown up", am I doing what God wants me to do?  Is God pleased with my labor?  The quest to answer such questions is one of life's greatest challenges for followers of Jesus.  Many people are dissatisfied, even disenchanted, on their vocational journeys.  They view employment as a necessary evil and wonder if God has a Plan Divine as they are stuck doing Plan Self.  Plan Self means doing what brings the most money and ease of life without consulting God to see if He has something else in mind.  *Plan Divine means regularly pursuing God's interests and not resting contentedly until you are absolutely sure you*

> **Plan Divine means regularly pursuing God's interests and not resting contentedly until you are absolutely sure you are firmly entrenched doing what He wants you to do.**

*are firmly entrenched doing what He wants you to do.* Plan Self often yields discontentment along with restlessness or even despair. Plan Divine always delivers peace that passes human comprehension.

I settled for Plan Self living during my first 15 years of post-college work. After the initial thrill of employment faded, the a.m. alarm clock was no longer welcomed enthusiastically, and I often wondered about my purpose in life. The 30-year retirement package, great wages, outstanding benefits and stocking up a 401K seemed alluring but were never satisfying.

As He sometimes does, God used a friend to ignite a spark in April 1994. That friend, Joseph Parker of Harrison County, Kentucky, challenged me to start a ministry that would take clothing, jobs and evangelism to the former Soviet Union. After an initial "NO-GO-BUT-THANK-YOU-JOE" reaction, the Lord showed me through friends and circumstances that He had chosen me. I could stall and make excuses, but I could not hide. Life became a whirlwind from the time of that challenge forward, but initial uncertainties turned into a mission ministry known as MASTER Provisions. A call against my will had begun!

*May this book encourage you to follow God's call on your life regardless of your age, income level, talents or any other excuse you hold so dearly!* Praise God! He changes lives and plans to fulfill His divine purpose! Are you hearing His call?

**May this book encourage you to follow God's call on your life regardless of your age, income level, talents or any other excuse you hold so dearly!**

*Part* 1

# A Change in Will

CHAPTER *1*

# Stubborn Years

A desperate mother in Kherson, Ukraine gave birth to Veronika and discarded her to die in a filthy outhouse reservoir. Amazingly, a passerby immediately heard the abandoned newborn's cries. That courageous lady fetched the baby from certain death and administered emergency medical treatment. Then, she delivered the precious cargo to a nearby orphanage. One year later, Veronika was adopted by a Christian family in Ukraine through the MASTER Care orphan placement ministry established by MASTER Provisions. Jesus said that pure and undefiled religion means taking care of orphans in their distress.

An eight-year old girl with worn out shoes walked into the clothing shop with her mother. The young mom was thrilled to find a pair of brand new shoes donated by someone from the Midwestern U.S. that fit her daughter perfectly. The little girl jumped up and down with excitement and jabbered gleefully in Russian. The mother was overcome with emotion and asked through tear-drenched eyes that the person who cared enough to donate these shoes receive her thanks. Surely, Jesus would provide clothing and shoes for needy people.

The young boy in Kosova witnessed hundreds of huge bags filled with clothing and many boxes of good shoes delivered to his mountain community in a shipping container. He asked, "Are these gifts from Allah?" "No," came the reply, "All of these gifts are from believers in Jesus!" For the next two days, that excited young man turned into an evangelist for Christ as he ran up and down the streets proclaiming that the clothing and shoes were gifts from believers in Jesus. Needy people hear about Jesus and receive badly needed clothing and shoes — evangelism through clothing ministries. WOW! What a powerful way to meet a basic physical need while teaching spiritual truth!

It is possible to care for physical and spiritual needs simultaneously. Indeed, many human necessities are met worldwide through ministries like MASTER Provisions. How did a "career telephone man" with a stubborn heart turn into the president of a dynamic organization that evangelizes while caring for orphans, distributing clothing and creating jobs in economically distressed countries?

The process began in the 1960's as I, Roger Babik, sat every week as a pew jockey at the Madeira Church of Christ in Cincinnati, Ohio. Particularly stirring mission sermons or presentations consistently yielded a thought: "I would like to be a preacher or missionary one day." That notion was securely hidden in the recesses of my gray matter, not to be shared with others. Not even my parents knew this secret desire. After the typically uninspiring slide show (always featuring a sunset shot finale) and some chitchat in the church foyer, Mom and Dad would host visiting missionaries as often as possible. We shared meals with people from almost every continent from my earliest childhood days. The personal contacts were always more interesting and informative than the slide shows. I became regularly exposed to the lives of full-time vocational Christian service workers.

The Babik family was always present for Wednesday night youth group, special events, revivals and Sunday night services. The trips to Frisch's Restaurant on Sunday nights after church were treasured and greatly anticipated dining experiences in the 60's and 70's. As a family, we were immersed in the work of the church and heavily involved in youth groups.

I enjoyed ample opportunities to learn about my areas of giftedness. Music ministry was not a viable option. Learning to play the accordion was a chore, and I refused to take piano lessons. Six years of regular accordion lessons is enough instrumental torture for a lifetime! Singing in front of others produced incredible fear and shyness in an otherwise gregarious person. The church folk politely endured the only solo performance of my life when I howled "Nobody Came" as the character, Waldo, in a teen musical. They even dug deep into their souls and fabricated compliments about my vocal abilities. Church people don't lie to you, do they? Perhaps that tactic could be classified as honorable deception. I knew what they were doing and enjoyed their kind words anyway.

Thoughts about a pastoral ministry, however, produced feelings exactly opposite of those generated by visions of music ministry. Preaching on Youth Sunday or talking in front of others always went well and never produced the tremendous anxiety normally associated with public speaking. Encouraging words about a message I delivered seemed more genuine because the task brought joy and fulfillment. Future speaking opportunities were always welcomed.

Involvement in sports absorbed lots of time during my formative years, especially in the high school days. Baseball, basketball and football at Madeira High School, along with summer baseball, consumed incredible blocks of time for four years. Perhaps visions of stardom, particularly in baseball, made it easier to conceal that inner calling towards full-time vocational Christian service. I was named first team all-city in Cincinnati after hitting .538 my senior year. Success at the state level in the American legion tournament made me think that perhaps baseball would hold some future hopes. Never mind that my speed was average and throwing inadequate — wouldn't it be great to play baseball in college?

During the summer of 1974, prior to my senior year of high school, we enjoyed a family vacation in North Carolina. As we started home, Mom mentioned that she once sang in Cincinnati Bible College's concert choir at Milligan College in East Tennessee. She suggested that it would be nice to stop by and visit the college. That's the first I had heard about Milligan, a Christian liberal arts college. Sure enough, I loved the scenic beauty of the region, and the school seemed like a great choice. There, I would have the opportunity to study in a Christian environment and maybe get a degree leading to full-time Christian service. (Or, maybe get to play college baseball. You see, I heard they had a fairly decent baseball program.) One of life's most difficult choices just became simplified, and I knew, Lord willing, what was going to transpire the first four years after high school.

It was late August 1975 and move-in day for all incoming freshmen at Milligan. I entered Webb Hall, a men's dormitory, and checked in with the Head Resident, Coach Duard Walker. I trucked up three floors to my assigned Room 313 with the first load of worldly possessions. On the trip down the old concrete stairs, I stopped and looked at the first guy rambling up towards me. For some strange reason I asked, "Are you Kevin?" Sure enough, it was Kevin Speas (who also had some hair at that time), the roommate that would share Webb 313 for four years. Lots of late night card games, laughter, and basketball road trips as co-managers for the Milligan Buff hoops squad and a few tears would mark our strong friendship. The sudden and unexpected death of Kevin's mother early in our college years allowed us to grow closer together as we walked through the valley of death's shadow.

Perhaps my fondest dorm memory, culinary archival division, came courtesy of Kevin's granny. She supplied us with incredibly delicious homemade, chunky peanut butter and grape jam to satisfy the late night hunger pangs associated with college life. Crackers coated with PB & J served as our collegiate snack du jour that we enjoyed together and shared with other dormitory freeloaders! Our ability to live together peacefully for four years with no arguments speaks volumes about Kevin's patience and good sense of humor. Unfortunately, we rarely shared on a deeper level about things that last forever. That had become my pattern: superficial living, going through the motions spiritually and suppressing God's call on my life.

The most important spiritual lesson I learned during the Milligan years actually came in conjunction with baseball. The lesson: *God wants us to include Him and glorify Him in every-*

*thing we do!* Buff Coach Harold Stout, somewhat of a legend in Tennessee coaching circles, welcomed me to fall tryouts in September 1975. He liked my abilities but did me a huge favor in a surprising manner. Coach Stout said I would make the team but ride the bench for two years behind an All-American caliber player, Ronnie Doss. So, he advised me to study hard, get good grades, play summer ball and then come back for tryouts my junior year. That initially crushing assessment ended with two great outcomes: straight A's for two years (except for one B my sophomore year) and plenty of time to meet a future Mrs. Babik. True to his word, Coach Stout warmly welcomed me back to the squad for my junior year, and I earned the starting job at first base. I was quick to internally take credit for this accomplishment, however, instead of giving thanks where thanks belonged. I suppose that God spared me the Herod quick-strike method for removing self-praisers because He wasn't finished with me yet. Instead, I received sorrows enough to drive any baseball player crazy. As the season began, everything I hit hard found a defender's glove. I returned from a very lackluster string of performances in Florida and glanced at the batting averages listed in the local paper: Babik, Milligan, .077. That's THREE hits in 39 official at bats. When your IQ is higher than your batting average, you are probably more qualified to sit as a spectator than play as a participant for your team. But, Coach Stout stuck with me.

That first night back in the dorm, I knelt before God and acknowledged that I had left Him out of my life. I was trying to

**God wants us to include Him and glorify Him
in everything we do!**

play baseball for my own personal recognition and glory. What's the use of that? Begging God's forgiveness, I vowed to pray to Him before and after every time at bat and give Him praise and honor regardless of what happened in every situation. That next day, our first home game after the spring trip, my baseball fortunes changed with three hits in four at bats. That was as many hits in one game as in the previous 13 games combined. I remembered to give God the thanks and praise for everything that happened every game, every at bat and every play. By season's end, our team record was 30-15, my batting average soared to .315 and my 41 RBI's (Runs Batted In — or runners that scored as a result of what you did as a batter) set a school record at that time. I learned to put God first in everything and give Him praise and thanks in all circumstances.

Baseball's spiritual lesson, unfortunately, was not enough to convict me to follow that hidden desire to pursue a Christian vocational career. So, instead of taking Bible and ministry courses, I yielded to the lure of money and a large salary and pursued courses in economics and business administration. *It's very easy to make life's choices based on money, power and prestige.* Those three things bring temporary gratification that deceives many people.

Upon graduation from Milligan in 1979, an elder at the Madeira church, Ray Weitzel, helped me to secure employment at Cincinnati Bell Telephone Company. My initial work assignment involved completing an internship and learning

. . . . . . . . . . . . . . . . . . . . . . . . . . . . . . . . . . . . . . . . .
**It's very easy to make life's choices based on
money, power and prestige.**
. . . . . . . . . . . . . . . . . . . . . . . . . . . . . . . . . . . . . . . . .

many different facets of Operator Services. After finishing the internship program, I was installed as a Supervisor of Long Distance Operators. All managers in that field, from the time of Alexander Graham Bell through the 70's, had been female. Young male college graduates assigned to supervise mostly female toll operators created quite a stir. Dealing with "women's issues" and learning a lot of practical personnel management skills were helpful. However, such experiences yielded little job satisfaction. Thus began a career in the business world marked by a definite lack of contentment and purpose in life.

After one year on the job, Tanya and I married on May 10, 1980, exactly one week before she graduated from Milligan. The Tennessee girl relocated to Northern Kentucky to start a new life. We learned a couple of good lessons about trusting God with our finances during the Cincinnati Bell days of the 80's. As newlyweds, we made the mistake of debt purchasing in the first year. With two incomes and no kids, it was easy to get caught in the trap of immediate acquisition through instant credit. Our home church, First Church of Christ (in Florence at that time and now thriving in Burlington), badly needed more parking, so they asked for offerings to expand the lot. *Both of us were taught to tithe, but offerings above the tithe represented new "trust" territory.* We had zero in the bank account and were awaiting pay day at month's end, but we decided to give $250 anyway the following Sunday. That Friday, we received an unexpected $253 check from an escrow account that had been established when we closed on

. . . . . . . . . . . . . . . . . . . . . . . . . . . . . . . . . . . . . . . . . . . . . . . .

**Both of us were taught to tithe, but offerings above the tithe represented new "trust" territory.**

. . . . . . . . . . . . . . . . . . . . . . . . . . . . . . . . . . . . . . . . . . . . . . . .

our first home. WOW! I'd never been so excited about a $3 surplus. God blessed that decision to make a sacrificial offering.

We experienced growth on the work and home fronts during the 1980's. I advanced through a series of assignments and promotions that ended with the job that brought the most enjoyment during my Cincinnati Bell Telephone years, Business Service Center Supervisor for commercial representatives. We were blessed at home with some baby Babiks during the latter half of that decade. Lydia entered the fold in April 1986, Jerrod joined ranks in September 1987 and Leah was launched in June 1989. God provided complication-free births and healthy babies. Tanya adapted quickly to her role as full-time mother and was exceptionally loving and nurturing.

In the fall of '89, First Church began a capital campaign to raise money for a new facility. Each family was asked to make a sacrificial gift to the Raising Stones of Witness campaign. Tanya had abandoned the special education teacher corps in '86 because of our commitment to keep her home to raise the little Babiks. Making a three-year commitment above the tithe on one relatively fixed income seemed overwhelming, but we settled on an initial offering of $5,000. After a final challenge by church leadership, Tanya and I prayed over the matter and agreed to give $7,500. We still did not fully realize how God longs for all of us to trust him totally with our finances.

Less than one month after making this three-year commitment as part of the campaign leadership team, I was asked to change jobs; actually told I would be moving to a new Account Executive sales position with major accounts. When it comes to personnel moves, corporations operate under a "tell, don't ask" policy, you know. However, God's plans were beautiful even though "I'd rather quit than do sales" was my first thought. I was actually enjoying the current work assignment and looking forward to continued personnel management, not working in sales. God was working ahead of me as I stumbled into the latter stages of negotiations on a huge telecommunications sale. Including the windfall bonus from that sale, my first quarterly commission check was the largest one I ever received, over $7,000. Jehovah Jireh! God Provides! Once again, *God reminded us about His providential care for those who choose to trust Him with everything.*

The Babik family numbered six when Joy arrived in December 1990. All signs on the surface pointed to a telecommunications career. Although I always liked working with people, I really did not enjoy the nature of the job itself. The great money and benefits eased the pain and made it easy to provide for a growing family. In addition to work duties, I served as a deacon, teen leader and Missions Committee member at First Church, got involved with officiating and coaching and still played softball two nights a week. On the outside, I appeared to be the most contented guy on the planet, but my inside feelings had never changed. In my mind, there was no significant purpose for selling communications products and services. For most people, including me, jobs in Corporate America were simply a means to make money and perhaps attain some level of earthly importance. The morning alarm clock initiated a snooze frenzy each day: how many times can you hit the snooze button and still get to work on time? I continued to avoid God's quiet, tender voice that beckoned me to serve Him in Christian ministry.

**God reminded us about His providential care for those who choose to trust Him with everything.**

In the early 90's, I remember more of an interest and eagerness to share my faith in Christ with those around me. The Sales Vice President entered my office to ask for a Scripture reference because he knew the Bible had a prominent position on my desk. I invited people like Vicki McClure to join us at First Church. That invitation led to the eventual dedication of her life to Christ. Years later, Vicki will still occasionally thank me for inviting her to church. Vicki and Gary McClure are great models of what married couples can do together to further the work of the Church. A young co-op student named Bill gave his life to Jesus over lunch one summer day as I explained the Gospel to him.

Most of all, I wished there was something more for me in life vocationally, but I seemed determined to have things my way with security in the status quo. *Fear of the unknown kept me from seeking God intently to see the plan He had in store for me.*

Back on our initial visit at the First Church of Christ, September 7, 1980, the first two people that Tanya and I met were Kenny Hicks, an extremely tall man, and his significantly more attractive bride, Linda. They invited us to a young married couple's class called the Merry Mates. It was the first Sunday for the class, which was led by a relatively young man, Joe Parker and his wife, Brenda. Lifelong friendships with the Hicks and the Parkers started that day even though Kenny envisioned me as a stuffed-shirt type with zero sense of humor. His errant first impression was based on my appearance wearing an outdated polyester suit and tie while displaying uncharacteristic seriousness.

**Fear of the unknown kept me from seeking God intently to see the plan He had in store for me.**

We started Thursday morning prayer breakfasts at Joe Parker's place in 1986, which continue today when Joe is in town. The menu is God-like, it never changes: sausage and egg biscuits, tomatoes (in season and home grown only featuring yellow and red varieties), orange juice and coffee. We invested many hours on Thursday mornings in prayer, Bible study and related conversation. We became close friends and trusted brothers in Christ.

Joe met a gentleman named Roger Denhart on a mission trip to Haiti in the late 1980's. A lasting friendship began amidst the poverty and trials of daily life in Haiti. A few years after the Caribbean adventure, Roger, a lifelong farmer and agricultural expert from Central Illinois, traveled to the Ukraine region of the USSR with Team Expansion. Team Expansion is a dynamic organization, led by Doug Lucas, that plants new churches and sends missionaries to areas of the world not yet reached with the Good News about Jesus.

In the summer of 1991, with the Soviet Communist government beginning to unravel, Team Expansion launched their work in Ukraine. They introduced a multi-faceted, Ukrainian-American Christian Friendship Festival to evangelize Ukrainians through films, lectures and English studies. The festival also enabled farmers like Roger Denhart to consult with agricultural specialists in order to share knowledge and also pray for the prairies of Ukraine. During the visit, Roger was impressed by the rich, black soil of Ukraine, the literal breadbasket of the former Soviet Union. Roger returned from the mission trip with great excitement and shared stories with us. After hearing from Mr. Denhart, Joe told him that they might start a farming operation in Ukraine if Communism ever fell. Joe always liked a challenge! By God's plan, Communist USSR swiftly fell a couple of months later in that land of rich soil and poor people. Ukraine became one of the 15 independent countries once part of the Soviet Union. It was not long before Roger reminded Joe of the possibility of starting a farm in Ukraine.

As a man who dreams God-sized visions and is not afraid to pursue them, Joe planned an initial visit to Ukraine with Roger Denhart to examine agricultural opportunities there in early 1992. The two farmers were welcomed cordially, and many Ukrainians wanted to learn about American farming practices. The novelty of hosting a couple of Americans, formerly not welcome on Ukrainian soil, was intriguing and exciting. Joe and Roger received royal treatment in every town they visited. Subsequent and frequent trips bathed in prayer and discussion of farming plans eventually led to the formation of a joint U.S.-Ukrainian agricultural venture known as Freedom Farm in 1992. Freedom Farm's objective was to deliver American equipment, expertise and methodology to Ukraine in order to increase crop yield and land productivity. The venture constituted high-risk, trailblazing activity not compatible with the timid soul. It's probably good that Joe could not foresee all of the turmoil and financial strain that would accompany such a bold initiative or the farming project and, subsequently, MASTER Provisions may never have developed.

Joe invested significant capital along with six months per year in Ukraine during the first two years of the business partnership. In May 1993, Joe mentioned that he had some ideas for us to help the people of Ukraine. I expressed very limited interest in that notion and banished the concept from further thought. I was not yet spiritually ready for the challenge.

Joe would invest four weeks in Ukraine, four weeks at home, back and forth. During each trip, Joe observed a tremendous need for clothing and jobs, and he noticed that Ukrainians were very eager to learn about Jesus and spiritual matters. Bibles and Christianity had been outlawed for over 70 years, and their new-found religious freedom offered great opportunities for mission work and evangelism.

Devout believers, like Nikolay Tatishvili, amazed the prospective cross-cultural farmers with their faith. Nikolay's car was old and mechanically unstable, like most vehicles there in the early 90's. Ukrainians could not afford simple things like replacement batteries. Nikolay's battery was absolutely worthless, so he would always try to park on an incline to jump-start the manual transmission car. However, Ukraine is predominately flat, and many times it is hard to find sloped ground. When that happened, everyone would cram into the car, and Nikolay would bow his head and pray fervently for quite a while. After prayer, he would turn the key, and God started the car with a dead battery every time. Surely, there were many things that our God could initiate in Ukraine — just like He started Nikolay's jalopy.

One Thursday morning, after prayer breakfast, as I prepared to travel to another day of work in downtown Cincinnati, Joe said that we needed to talk. He wanted to discuss the ideas that we briefly broached a year earlier. Mostly, he needed to talk. My task was to listen. We set a time to meet that weekend in early April 1994. I was not totally aware of the topic for our discussion but was always willing to listen when Joe had an idea. Joe Parker is a Mr. E.F. Hutton (renowned financial adviser in the '80s who received great attention when he spoke) to me in spiritual matters.

## Lessons Learned During The Stubborn Years

- *Distractions are always present to keep you from clearly discerning God's higher plans for your life. For me, the distractions often took the form of sports.*
- *You can be used greatly by God in any job, whether the actual work brings satisfaction or not.*
- *God prepares you for the future through past experiences.*
- *Listen to older, respected people.*
- *God wants you to enjoy your life's labor.*
- *Look for God to provide an opportunity for you to work vocationally in your areas of competence and enjoyment.*
- *God wants you to develop the talents and skills that bring you joy and satisfaction.*
- *The more time you spend with God, the more you hear from Him through people, circumstances and His Word.*
- *Trust God with your money and give liberally to His work. Give more than the tithe.*

CHAPTER *2*

# The Call and Homework

Joe Parker shared his burden with me for the people of Ukraine. In fact, every time he returned from a working trip, Joe mentioned the need for clothing and jobs. Moreover, a tremendous interest in spiritual matters was evident everywhere he traveled in that country of fifty million people. Ukrainians expressed a desire to know more about Jesus in the face of disastrous economic conditions. Unbelievably high inflation had ravaged the nation in less than two years. Can you imagine 3,500 percent inflation in less than two years? In other words, three thousand five hundred dollars in your bank account became worth ONE dollar in less than 24 months. Unemployment was high, wages were low and the cost of goods was high. A pound of meat could be purchased for two day's wages. Clothing became nearly unaffordable for the average Ukrainian. A strong sense of financial desperation seized the newly independent country. The needs were enormous.

*God often uses others as His mouthpieces,* and Joe called to me on God's behalf that day with a simple question: "Roger, are you willing to start a ministry that would meet clothing needs, create jobs and take the Gospel of Jesus Christ to the people of Ukraine?" To be sure, there was no immediate Isaiah-like response such as "Here am I, send me."

I sat quietly to absorb the magnitude of that question. The normally articulate and verbose balding one remained silent. After a while, I responded with some questions. The questions represented a litany of excuses. "Why would I want to help people in Ukraine that I never met?" "When do I have time to start a mission outreach with all that is going on in my life: Chairman of Missions Committee, Deacon and Sunday School teacher at First Church, full-time employee at Cincinnati Bell and coach of the kids' ball teams?" "How could I still play softball this year?" "Who could possibly ever get such a mission started?" My initial reaction displayed a continued unwillingness to follow God's call even if He were to personally write out His plan for my life, invite me to a mountaintop and present the directive on a gold-embossed marble tablet. My answer was "NO!" Certainly, it was an honor to be considered for this task. However, this was not the right time for me to consider such a work.

Never one to take rejection at face value, Joe simply asked that Tanya and I pray about this opportunity to assist people and spread the Good News in Ukraine...and, pray about this for one month. Grudgingly, I agreed to pray about the request during the rest of April, and we would reconvene in early May. "Maybe

**God often uses others as His mouthpieces.**

Tanya won't even be interested in praying about this." I thought. That would be the easy way out since I could just tell Joe that WE were not interested in pursuing this vision.

Tanya is given to prayer, so it was not a problem for her to devote a month in prayer to such an unusual call. Even though she said she would never marry a preacher (or missionary for that matter), she joined me in prayer during April 1994. After all, even if we were to do this work, it would probably just be a short-term project and then we would return to life as normal. *If you want to make time seem to pass more slowly, earnestly pray every day about something for a month.* April '94 seemed like forever!

During the four weeks of prayer, two interesting things happened at Cincinnati Bell Telephone Company. First, several people I had worked with for years made comments about how they noticed that it seemed like I really was not enjoying my job lately. Certainly, I was more pensive than ever, because I was dwelling constantly on the mission opportunity at hand. No matter the reason, they had never made such comments before.

The most notable circumstance transpired at our Annual Sales Rally held in late April at a swanky downtown hotel. The purpose of the rally was to motivate us to higher achievements and to recognize accomplishments. The keynote speaker was a renowned mountain climber; one of the most inspiring public speakers I had ever heard. It's too bad I do not remember his name, because I would love to hear him speak again. One of his lifelong goals was to climb to the peak of Mt. Everest. He described

**If you want to make time seem to pass more slowly, earnestly pray every day about something for a month.**

that challenge as his passion and calling in life. At great length, he recalled the arduous preparations for the high adventure and the journey itself. An incredible amount of physical training and sacrifice was required in order to have a chance to endure the rigorous ascent. They hired native Sherpas to assist in the trek, and he relived the emotional trauma they experienced as part of their expeditionary team perished in the dangerous climb. With God's help, he was able to accomplish the incredible feat of conquering Mt. Everest.

The speech was indeed riveting, but his words at the end were the very words of God to me. "If you don't enjoy what you are doing here at Cincinnati Bell, you need to do something different. Follow your passion!" "OK, God, you win," I thought as he closed the speech. If you can get your message out through a donkey, you can surely speak through a prolific mountain climber.

After the month of prayer, I shared the news with Joe that I was willing to help on the mission project for Ukraine. So, we sat down to discuss the venture in detail. I entered the meeting viewing myself as a volunteer and holding on to the concept that I would be at Cincinnati Bell "'til retirement do us part". So, what happens when you volunteer to do a job? Of course, you have homework! Joe's visionary mind had already kicked into gear so he laid out my initial three jobs: 1) name the mission organization; 2) figure out how to collect tons upon tons of good used clothing and shoes; and 3) write an evangelical tract to distribute with the clothing. For his part, Joe's homework mandated a meeting with Ukrainian church leaders to determine how to turn a shipment of used clothing and footwear into a viable ministry outreach.

Homework — Part Two seemed fairly easy. God's people enjoy doing God's work, so we should partner with churches to complete the bulk of the clothes collection. Now parts one and three represented formidable challenges requiring some brain-work, making them candidates for procrastination. We actually started collecting clothing in May before the mission was named. Joe's garage became Service Center Number One. There was no room for vehicles in the Parker garage during the summer of 1994.

The most urgent assignment was to name our mission so that we could complete required paperwork and apply for incor-poration as a not-for-profit organization. The pressure mounted as May slipped away. The Wednesday night before Memorial Day, I laid down for a night's recharge and was awakened with a recurring thought as I dozed into "La-La Land". That thought was, *"Genesis 22, Genesis 22, Genesis 22"*. I wasn't sure what to think, so I got out of bed and read one of the great faith chapters of the Bible, Genesis, Chapter 22. It's the account of Abraham, and the first-born test of faith God literally laid out on an altar. At the very moment that Abraham reached out to slay his son, the angel of the Lord called out to Him from heaven. The pro-ceedings were temporarily suspended until God provided the substitute sacrifice, and verse 14 tells us that Abraham named that place The Lord Will Provide. That phrase repeated in my mind: The Lord Will Provide, The Lord Will Provide. Hey, that's it: "MASTER Provisions!" God had given a name in honor of the faith of Abraham and with assurance that He is a good MASTER who provides. We decided to capitalize every letter in MASTER in tribute to God's greatness. After all, He is a **BOLD GOD!**

Spring quickly slid into summer, and all of the necessary paperwork was completed so that MASTER Provisions could be established as an officially recognized not-for-profit organization. I scheduled appearances at five churches in Northern Kentucky and Cincinnati, and Joe Parker would speak for five minutes during morning worship services as I listened and learned about life in Ukraine. We prepared for a first shipment in August, but homework assignment number three had not been completed. I needed to compose a Gospel tract.

For two months, I had been jotting down thoughts and Biblical references as they came to mind. However, there was no real progress toward completion of the tract. On a mid-July Wednesday night, I was again drifting off to sleep. God woke me up. Perhaps I listen to God most clearly on Wednesday nights. Within two hours, the tract in its completed form was written and ready to send to Ukraine to be printed in Russian. Within two weeks, sixty thousand of the original tracts were published to hand out to people who received clothing. Assignment number three was completed just in time.

Joe moved forward with his assigned task and scheduled a meeting with the leaders at Kherson Christian Church in Kherson, Ukraine. He let them know that a seemingly capable sucker (I mean volunteer) had been located. On Joe's next trip overseas, he conducted several meetings to talk about starting a clothing ministry outreach in Ukraine.

Rather than taking our American methods overseas, Joe asked for Ukrainian leadership to develop guidelines and procedures to establish a clothing mission. They decided to give away clothing to eight classes of people: widows, orphans, disabled, homeless, seniors on fixed incomes, families with many children, prisoners and disaster victims. The rest of the clothing would be priced in line with low wages and sold at thrift shops conveniently located throughout the city. Proceeds from clothing sales would be used to cover all wages and delivery expenses, and any profits would be used to further God's work at Kherson Christian Church. A manager for the work would be chosen from the church family, and many unemployed believers could finally have a good job at a Christian clothing shop. Workers would be able to tell customers about Jesus Christ. Christian music could be played for all to hear, and evangelical tracts, Bibles and New Testaments could be given to people who wanted to know more. CLOTHING, JOBS and EVANGELISM, the three-in-one of MASTER Provisions: an exciting missions concept was born!

## So, how do you know when God is making a call on your life?

*Here are some telltale signs to help you know when God is calling you to do something for Him:*

- *When God calls, He often uses other people to make the call and to confirm the calling.*
- *When God calls, He sovereignly ordains circumstances that help to clarify His desires for you.*
- *When God calls, He provides a warm reassurance of what He desires for your life.*
- *When God calls, Satan will try to distract you and tempt you to procrastinate or decline the call altogether.*
- *When God calls, He will be patient as He waits for your decision.*
- *When God calls, you will not feel pressured to make a hasty decision.*

- *When God calls, He does not offer all of the details in advance, thereby testing your faith in Him.*

# CHAPTER 3

# Happy Birthday, MASTER Provisions!

Birthdays are easy to determine, albeit sometimes difficult to remember. No parent can ever forget the exhilaration and joy associated with their child's date of arrival to Earth. We remember with great delight the first time we gently cradled God's special little gift to us. We never forget, or at least hope we never forget, the child's birthday. That cherished day is a fixed date now and forever. For mission organizations, however, the date of birth is not so easy to calculate. Was it the day the idea was first conceived in Joe's mind? Or, perhaps the day we sat down to discuss how to bring the organization into being? Was it the day that the first bag of clothing was donated by a lady in the Villages of Beechgrove? Or, maybe the day we filed for incorporation? Was it the day that God planted the name in my weary mind? Or, how about a more apropos question? Does the birthday really matter? NO. However, so that you may have an annual opportunity to send birthday greetings (or gifts), we will use the date that our filing as a charitable organization was accepted by the Commonwealth of Kentucky. Happy Birthday to MASTER Provisions on June 20, 1994 (a good date in a good state)!

The birth of a mission brings a lot of growth challenges. My biggest personal challenge involved learning to balance home life, spiritual life, work life, church life and mission life while maintaining essential relationships in each area. Personal time management became more critical than ever as a very worthy, yet time-consuming, task was added to an already hectic life. The excitement of a new challenge made it easier to get up and at 'em extra early. People at work actually noticed my new enthusiasm for life, but I tried to hide the new avocation from them. I did not want to let others know prematurely about this volunteer activity for fear of any negative reactions. During the initial months of growth, I still had no idea of what the future held and no thought of leaving employment at Cincinnati Bell.

Almost every weekend in June and July, we launched a clothing drive at a Northern Kentucky or Greater Cincinnati area church. Launching a drive simply meant arranging with a church to allow us to give a four to five minute "Mission Moment" during morning worship services so that Joe could share about the needs in Ukraine. I just tagged along each week to listen and interact with church folk after the services. The piles of clothing donated at each church in two weeks following Joe's presentation were remarkable. We scheduled pick-ups at the churches and then transported the donated shoes and clothing to Joe's garage. Saturdays and evenings became work times when we recruited volunteers to help us sort and pack the clothing to prepare it for shipment. Kenny Hicks suggested we try using some extra large and tough plastic bags that were packing materials discarded as trash by an adjacent business in the Florence Industrial Park. Sure enough, the bags worked well to pack 80-85 pound oblong bales, approximately forty inches tall, which were stacked in the garage. Joe was not sure that the garage floor, which also doubled as the cistern ceiling, would accommodate the tons of weight that had accumulated. It was time to seek warehouse space!

The very first businessman that Joe contacted, Mr. Shirley Elliott, ran the Boone-Kenton Warehouse, located less than a mile from Joe's home. Shirley was incredibly gracious and gave us some floor space near the loading dock. Gradually, we transitioned operations from Joe's garage to the BK warehouse. The stack of completed bags seemed enormous to us near the end of July 1994.

We had never packed goods in a 40-foot long shipping container and had no idea how many bags of clothing and boxes of shoes it would take to fill one. We calculated cubic footage within a container and cubic footage of the pile at the warehouse and felt that we had plenty to fill the first container by mid-August. Determining cubic footage for a pile of large, rounded bags is a "guesstimation" rather than a science, and we thought that no single shipping container could hold everything in that stack. Accordingly, we scheduled the first loading date late in the afternoon on Monday, August 15.

We completed the job with only six men, and we were all exhausted from the effort. Jerrod especially enjoyed frolicking on top of the clothes mountain while rolling bags down to the loaders. We learned that by using leg power to squish the clothing, you could get six bags across on each row instead of just five. We had not allowed for the "squish factor" when estimating cubic footage of load material, so we realized toward the end of the day that we would have some empty space at the back of the container. Joe's wife, Brenda, and Tanya hurriedly motored over to the Dollar Store and bought a large quantity of cereal to fill in the empty space. The first container in MP history was ready to sail!

The next morning at work, the district manager came into my office and said he saw a really nice photo and article in the newspaper about my involvement with MASTER Provisions. Now that was news to me, but I did not know if it was good or bad news. Sure enough, the *Kentucky Post* had run a front-page story including a color photo of Joe and me helping to load the clothing container. Oops, the cat was officially released from the bag as far as keeping my involvement in the mission endeavor a secret. Actually, the management at CBT was very supportive of the work since they placed a high value on community involvement and volunteer service. Amazingly, people got excited about the fact that they could donate gently used clothing and shoes to MASTER Provisions.

The newspaper exposure generated a lot of interest among area churches and individuals and was certainly a catalyst for rapid growth. The pace of donations increased rapidly as did the amount of volunteer work needed to process donated items. We did not yet realize that churches would be willing and able to help sort and pack the goods they had donated. We had that "rather do it ourselves" mentality that limits growth and wears out bodies. Thank God for faithful friends like Allen McClaskey, Kenny Hicks, Scott Crissinger, Bob Mayo and David and Nathan Madden who were willing to help pack clothes regularly during our first year of existence.

Through God's grace and bounty, we were able to complete two more shipments in '94: one in October and another in

December. We learned a lesson in clothes work from the October load — never lay your own clothing anywhere near the work area. Ralph Wilmhoff, one of our early container loaders, got heated up during the festivities, so he peeled off his jacket and laid it down inside the container on that chilly October day. An incoming bag burst totally. We scooped up everything in sight and, unknowingly, included Ralph's nice hardware store jacket in the repacked bag. As we finished the load and prepared to head home, Ralph searched the warehouse to find his missing coat. Immediately, we knew what had happened. Ralph had donated a jacket!

We learned to never undress anywhere near the work area and have reminded people often not to repeat that mistake. Unfortunately for the unwitting givers, there have been other "Ralphs" on the job over the years. The most "bizarre and valuable unintended gift" award surely belongs to Jolene Elliott. While packing clothing in Arizona, her diamond wedding ring was accidentally dislodged as she slid her hand down the side of the bag. About thirty minutes later, she noticed the ring was missing. We unpacked all of the bags that were suspected carriers of the diamond but could not find the ring. In addition, we marked a big "X" on those same bags. Our friends in Ukraine double-checked them after the shipment arrived overseas, but we never did find Jolene's ring. She took the loss quite well, in part, because she is a missionary and formerly worked in Ukraine. Most importantly, Jolene's heart is not set on earthly things, even something as precious as a wedding ring. A few parents have come unglued a tad when junior left his designer coat in the work area and could not find it at clean up time. But, it's usually a good source for laughter. Most folks don't get too frosted over inadvertently donated items, because they realize that people overseas have needs much greater than their own.

As we evaluated operations and growth of MASTER Provisions in our birth year at the inaugural board meeting in December, we were amazed at the steady growth and interest. Churches were already lining up to help as 1994 faded into '95. Even churches that helped the first year were prepared for round two. Surely, we thought, people would not have any clothing or shoes left to donate, what with the huge pile of items they collected last year. We would address naked churchgoers in succeeding years if we conducted annual clothing drives. WRONG! That theory has been shattered year after year at many churches around the Midwest U.S. "Me thinketh we shoppeth too much", but our clothing abundance has served as a source of blessing and provision for millions of people overseas!

A shipment every other month was planned for 1995, and it became increasingly difficult to manage the rapid growth of MASTER Provisions. Joe suggested that I make a mission trip to Ukraine with him towards the end of March 1995, to see firsthand the results of our efforts at home. Now that was a somewhat threatening proposition to me. I had never left the comfortable confines of America and never even taken a mission trip in the States. After talking with Tanya, we agreed that the trip would be good even though the timing seemed bad. The local airport was purchasing our home in Burlington, and we were scheduled to move in April. In addition to everything else on the work platter, many long evenings were spent remodeling the new Babik residence in Walton. Several times, I fell asleep exhausted on the floor amidst construction debris instead of returning to Burlington for a normal night of rest.

Perhaps two weeks of vacation time to travel to Ukraine would be the perfect way to slow down and celebrate the first year of volunteer service with MASTER Provisions. After all, it had been almost one full year since Joe approached me with the concept of beginning an outreach ministry to assist people in Ukraine.

CHAPTER 4

# Foreign Decision

When you head abroad for the first time, you must take care of travel details galore. I applied for my passport in February, and Joe took care of the visa, airline tickets and all other logistical issues. March 28, 1995, arrived with a mixed sense of nervousness and excitement: nervousness about temporarily leaving behind a wife and four young children and excitement about a first-time life experience. People at work were intrigued by the vacation purpose and destination, and I was fairly surprised by the amount of attention received from many people. I was still holding on to the idea that MASTER Provisions was my volunteer service, one that would eventually subside or be handed off to a "real missionary". Not once had I viewed this trip as a potentially life-changing experience.

The journey offered a much-needed respite from a year of intense activity and corresponding lack of sleep. It was difficult to unwind immediately. In fact, I was rather uptight during travel and even remember indigestion battling my innards as lunch was served on the final flight leg from London to Kiev, Ukraine. It's a long, grueling trip to wander through seven time zones and lose a night of sleep in the process. Joe was a routine patron of that airline route and served as a great travel companion and adviser. I recall a friendly wager about what would be served for one of the meals en route. The menu selection of beans and franks for breakfast sounded so bizarre that I unwisely deemed it an impossible option. The loss of that little contest cost me an insignificant amount to be recouped on a future golf trip, but that was the only unpleasant memory of the journey.

We arrived in Odessa, Ukraine, on March 29, and red tape took on a new meaning. After a couple of hours spent standing in lines to clear passport control and customs, we met our Ukrainian hosts outside of the airport. The hosts were friendly, smiling and talkative, in sharp contrast to the crowds of people. Almost everyone seemed so quiet, serious, even depressed — they wouldn't make eye contact.

During the initial trip, I realized that you could immediately identify Christians by the peace and joy that exuded from their lives, the radiant countenance on their faces and their inherent friendliness. Most buildings stood in various stages of disrepair and 3D took on a new meaning where each D stood for the condition of nearly everything: dark, dirty, and dilapidated. They whisked us off on a 4-hour car ride to a small apartment in Kherson, a city of 400,000 people in South Central Ukraine. Much of the first week was invested in observing the clothing operations and meeting new friends such as Sergey Kavetsky, interpreter extraordinaire. Mr. "Corvette-sky", as he calls himself, is always one of the funniest people alive. You're certain to enjoy the following Sergey stories.

Sergey showed me around his hometown of Kherson and let me observe all of the clothing work that had begun. We met all of the gracious people who were so glad to have nice jobs that actually allowed them to receive a salary. The first trip to the primary clothing warehouse was a treat. It was a maintenance-deprived, unheated building that welcomed all incoming shipments. Piles of clothing bags and shoe boxes packed and loaded by our loving friends back home were stacked neatly to the ceiling. At lunchtime, Sergey told me to wait and he would bring back some food from the market. So, I explored the warehouse, whistling as I wandered. In a few moments, a portly and elderly building guard started yelling at me and shaking her finger in the universal "No" manner. I raised my eyebrows and continued walking the floor, whistling as I strolled. The guard approached a second time shouting "Nyet, Nyet, Nyet" (No, No, No) with the veins sticking out of her neck. Her face was red, and she was obviously angry. I decided to literally hold tight, stop walking and keep breathing only to the extent necessary for survival until Sergey returned. The carefree Mr. Corvette-sky sauntered back with lunch in a few minutes. In somewhat panicked fashion, I informed him that the guard was apparently miffed by my existence. My dear interpreter friend asked me what I was doing to cause such problems. I responded with a sincere "I don't know." Without batting an eye, Sergey responded, "Well, whatever you don't know that you were doing, don't do it!" Such comic relief became expected of Sergey, one who has become a great friend and brother in Christ. I later learned of a Ukrainian wives' tale indicating that whistling indoors brings a curse on the building inhabitants: that they would make no money. It seemed like Ukraine had already received that curse whether I whistled or not, but I learned not to whistle indoors from my first cross-cultural missions blunder.

Mr. Kavetsky is not only funny, but also faithful. One of the most refreshing aspects of working with people from other cultures is that they do not operate in the rush mode like we do. One evening, as my valor overcame discretion and common sense, I told Sergey that I knew my way around the city pretty well. Well enough, I thought, to catch a bus and meet him at a stop near his home the following morning. I started earlier than usual on that rainy day in order to allow for any delays. The first bus I caught took an unexpected route and bypassed the stop where Sergey was waiting. So, I disembarked and caught a second bus, which finally got me to Sergey ninety minutes after our agreed-upon meeting time. Ukrainian buses are jam-packed and, as the doors opened, I waved at Sergey, who had been standing patiently in the rain for over an hour. However, in my politeness, the push of people to board led to that fatal error of failure to "de-bus" prior to take off. So, I pushed my way to the rear exit doors and jumped off at the next bus stop and ran 1/4 mile to meet the drenched Sergey Kavetsky. The amazing thing to me was that he was not upset. During a 90-minute wait, I would have looked at my watch so many times I'd be cross-eyed. In contrast, Sergey was laughing about not needing to take a shower for the next week. What grace! What a great and loyal friend!

Over the years, we enjoyed many opportunities to evangelize on the streets of Ukraine together on summer mission trips. Occasional thunderstorms onto poorly maintained roads lacking drainage sewers often caused lakes to form in the middle of streets. One morning, we were strolling down the roadways of Kakhovka after overnight storms. Sergey joked about how he was the iron man of all translators. He walked ahead as he looked back at me shouting, "I AM IRON MAN!" As the words iron and man left his lips, he faced forward at the very moment that he stepped into a puddle over 6 inches deep. His tennis shoes were soaked, but he immediately responded with a smile and quipped, "I am RUSTY man!" We still laugh about the incident that proves the Biblical principle that pride goes before a fall, or step, into the puddle.

Near the end of the 2004 summer trip, we enjoyed one of the most memorable overnight bus rides in the history of mission travel, courtesy of Sergey Kavetsky. The slaphappy team of 36 was crammed onto a 60's model bus for the 11-hour jaunt from Kakhovka to Kiev. Sergey decided that it would be the proper time to inform passengers about previously ignored Ukrainian travel etiquette rules. At that time, "real" toilets were at a premium along many roads, so you had to improvise. Sergey spontaneously issued a list of do's and don'ts for use of roadside "facilities". The list included, but was not limited to, the following:

- No more than three ladies per tree.
- Please limit all trips to two minutes or less unless stage fright occurs.
- Men use the east side and ladies use the west side of the highway.
- Walk far away for number two visits.
- Take care of business at least five feet away from all young trees.
- Do not talk to strangers while using the facilities.
- Do not use shiny leaves for clean up.
- Smile! You may be on candid camera!
- Use "flush lights" discreetly.

- Please return to the bus silently so that others may concentrate on pressing matters.

Everyone on the bus was laughing raucously by the time the rules clinic ended. Indeed, a classic moment in missions travel had transpired!

On the trip from downtown Kiev to the airport, an unforgettable practical joke had been preplanned. Only David Walker, a team member from Clearwater, Florida, and I knew the plan details. David had brought walky-talkies to use on the trip, and Sergey was absolutely fascinated with them. He envisioned using them with his young son, Andrew, and would pick one unit up and pretend like he was talking to him. Near the conclusion of the trip, David gave Sergey the walky-talkies. I got up in front of the whole busload of team members and made a scene, declaring that the walky-talkies belonged to me and David had no right to give them to Sergey. I acted mad and yelled at David. Everyone on the bus got stone silent. They had not seen me act like such an unreasonable fool before. I imagine they were thinking something like: "Here's our 'great' trip leader acting like a moron and hurting our beloved interpreter's feelings in front of everyone." Sergey immediately handed the walky-talkies back to me and sat down with the saddest, puppy-dog looking face you've ever seen. I couldn't maintain this facade very long, so I stood back up and asked Sergey to join me. We then presented him with an actual cell phone. Sergey was overjoyed! Then, I told him about the fabricated walky-talkie story, and David presented the units to Sergey as a gift so he could use them to play with Andrew. How wonderful to see Sergey go from completely dismayed to totally thrilled in the course of five minutes!

During the initial mission trip to Ukraine, I enjoyed the lengthy Sunday worships and meeting many new friends. On weekdays, Joe left the apartment early each morning. As a result, I had plenty of time for private Bible study, meditation and prayer prior to Sergey's arrival. The whole experience of visiting a country that was so poor and seeing incredible needs everywhere was very emotionally draining. I finally understood Joe's passion for bringing the Gospel, clothing and jobs to Ukraine. *At home, I had merely talked to people second-hand about the needs that now touched me face-to-face.* On Wednesday morning, in the middle of the trip, I was overcome by emotions during my quiet time with God. A strong conviction came over me that I had been running away from God's call all of my life. I had squelched those inner desires about being a preacher or missionary for over 30 years now. My preference had been to stay comfortable and do things Roger Babik's way. I wasn't open to God's Plan Divine for my life. I had settled for Plan Self. Kneeling alone on the floor of that small Ukrainian apartment, emotions overwhelmed me. I began to weep and shudder, crying out to God: "Lord, forgive me for my stubborn ways and pride. Forgive me for wanting to do things my way. Lord, take me and accomplish your purposes through me. I'll do what you want me to do."

After the emotional encounter with God, I immediately felt a peace that I had never before experienced. Roger had surrendered; God had control! The rest of the trip zoomed by as we continued our daily visits in the community. It was hard to wipe

**At home, I had merely talked to people second-hand about the needs that now touched me face-to-face.**

the smile off my face that reflected the joy in my heart. I couldn't wait to get home and share this "foreign" decision with Tanya and a close circle of friends. It was such a wonderful feeling to know that, at age 38½, for the very first time, God's call was no longer against my will.

*Part* 2
# Life in His Will

# CHAPTER 5

# Preparations Begin Amidst Doubters

Joe and I had plenty of time to share current experiences and future plans during the voyage home. It was like solitary confinement to be in Ukraine as far as world news is concerned. Actually, that's pretty refreshing. Sitting at Heathrow Airport in London, we learned of the tragic events at Oklahoma City that had unfolded while we were away from the States. The sobering reality of evil in the world and the reminder that every country is a mission field made its mark on my soul. I wanted to prepare to serve God daily as a missionary.

It was an exciting and blessed reunion as Tanya and the four young Babiks exchanged hugs and tears at the Greater Cincinnati/ Northern Kentucky International Airport on April 11. We actually arrived home hours ahead of our original schedule to their surprise. Boy, was it good to see the family. That's really the only thing I missed during the time abroad. Not the money, not the possessions, not the job; just the people I love so much! Our official move into the new home took place one week before the trip — brilliant domestic planning! I had left behind stacks of boxes everywhere. Some good friends transplanted trees and shrubs from the old homestead. Amidst the chaos of a physical move and the excitement of a new vocational commitment, where do you start discussions with your wife?

Tanya shared first about all of the domestic issues affecting the children, ages 4-8 at the time. We shared on an intimate level about the heartbrokenness I experienced in the mission field and the desire to move into full-time service with MASTER Provisions. The tremendous growth MP was experiencing required an increased time commitment. From a practical survival standpoint, there would be no way to manage a growing ministry plus keep up with work at Cincinnati Bell and maintain relationships at home and church. But, how do you move from secular employment making a very substantial income with incredible healthcare benefits into full-time mission work with low wages and no medical benefits? It does take a lot of money to take care of a family of six in our culture.

I returned to work at Cincinnati Bell with "the smile that had no end". People were curious about the trip and most listened intently or, at least, politely to the short version of my first mission trip experience. I dared not share the strong feeling that mission work was for me and my days at CBT were numbered. No one at work realized what I was going through internally, because corporate folk normally interpret constant happiness and enthusiasm as job satisfaction. Much to my amazement, I was promoted to a higher level Sales position in mid-year 1995. Pay and commission opportunities increased and actual work time involvement decreased since I had more support resources. It was easy to recognize God at work in this promotion. He knew more discretionary time was needed each day, and the job advancement enabled that to occur. Or, as the enemy's thoughts countered, was this promotion a sign that I was supposed to continue my corporate career? Those conflicting thoughts badgered me often. *Spiritual battles are often intense, and our enemy does not give up easily!*

It was time to give up playing softball and officiating basketball. Personal hobbies or avocations just needed to wait during this particular season of life. Quitting softball was not so hard. I notified the coach that I would not be playing that year, but he called to ask me to sub the very first week. I knew that subbing one week could easily turn into a six-month commitment. So, I graciously declined the offer and my softball career ended quietly. Getting yelled at by upset coaches, fans and parents that winter at basketball games was easy to give up. Consequently, officiating officially ended for me that year, as well.

Our family had started attending cell group meetings hosted by Community Christian Church that same spring of my first mission trip. Community was a new church being planted in Florence at the time when First Church was moving to its new facilities in nearby Burlington. The concept of the cell church appealed to us, so we contemplated helping to get this new work started since our home church was moving further away from our residence in Walton. We began to host cell group meetings, and I was asked to participate in leadership. We began worshiping

**Spiritual battles are often intense, and our enemy does not give up easily!**

and working with Community. That fall, Pastor Dan Monahan asked me if I had ever considered full-time Christian ministry. Hmmm? As a matter of fact, that interest had been planted in me as a child. I told Dan about my life's journey and the many times I heard God's higher calling, yet stubbornly refused to listen.

Thoughts about moving into full-time mission work moved to front and center each day. As I mentioned the possibility of this career change with close friends, nearly everyone had the same recommendation: why not ask churches and individuals to support you in this work? "Never thought of that", was my usual response. Heeding their advice, I began to approach friends and churches with the challenge for full-time missions that God had put on my heart and asked them to support the work financially. Since they were already familiar with MASTER Provisions and knew my capabilities and interests, people were eager to help. Even though we had chosen to serve at Community Christian, First Church's mission team recommended that they be our first supporter. First Church has been so faithful in so many ways! Fifteen other churches and individuals supported us that first year. We gathered money in reserve at MP and began to see how God planned to work out the practical details for a permanent transition into missions.

Near year-end, 1995, Dan asked me to pray about joining the staff at Community as a part-time associate. The transition plan continued to come together. Part-time work at Community Christian would replace full-time employment at Cincinnati Bell, and MASTER Provisions would become my main job. Everything seemed sensible, but some doubts surfaced. In fact, some sources of questioning were predictable, while others caught me by surprise. I could feel the spiritual attacks of Satan compounding as the Babiks greeted New Year, 1996. "Were you thinking about taking care of your family when you made that commitment to follow God's call? Shouldn't you wait until the children are older? Won't Tanya need to go back to work to help support the family?" Me thought that Satan asketh too many questions too often!

Concerned parents became classified as Doubters, Type A. There's something about the love and care of parents when there are grandchildren involved. My parents and in-laws both questioned the decision to leave CBT with respectful regularity. They had great reservations about the wisdom of such a move. Even though they indicated that they would support us unconditionally, they wanted us to make sure that we considered all the ramifications of the decision. If things don't work out, corporations are not usually willing to take people back. It really boiled down to a "stage of life" issue since we had four young children. So, did this mean that God could take care of Tanya and me, but it might be asking a bit much for God to care for a family of six? Of course not, but isn't that what we are saying when we question timing in relation to obeying God's call?

Well-intending co-workers filled the Doubters, Type B category. Obviously, you have to be very careful whom you trust in a corporate environment. There were a handful of people that had earned my trust over the years. I asked them what they thought about my desire to leave CBT. All but one felt it was a very miscalculated risk to leave the "security" of the telephone company for the uncertainties inherent in mission work. "Why not continue to volunteer with MP and find someone else who could eventually take your place in running that mission?" seemed like the overall consensus question. When Abram was asked to leave the comforts of his homeland and everything he knew, did he ask for someone else to take his place on the journey?

Concerned friends achieved Doubters, Class C status. They made comments like "You're crazy to leave a good job" and asked questions such as "Why do you want to depend on others for support?" Some friends were obviously opposed to the move from corporate America to full-time missions service. Doubts were invariably related to money matters. I had invested quite a few years living in that "doubt world", so I took no offense at any of the expressed concerns.

Tanya was resolute in her desire to see me follow God's call come what may. She understood the risks and doubts associated with life in ministry. After all, she was raised as a preacher's kid. Her father, Rodney, was a youth minister and camp director for years. From her mother, Billie, she learned the sacrifices required from a marriage partner. So, Tanya fully understood the selflessness and trials associated with family life in full-time Christian service. During college years, she said she was not going to marry a preacher and her wishes were granted. She did not marry a preacher; she married a missionary. To be precise, she married a "call-avoiding" businessman who was led by the Lord to become a missionary. Divorce never was, nor ever will be, an option for us, and Tanya committed to stand beside me no matter what. God, the ultimate grantor of the heart's desire, was faithful in not allowing Tanya to marry a preacher!

We shipped 8 containers to Ukraine in 1995 and 12 shipments were planned for 1996. Evenings and weekends were filled with clothes activities. Joe Parker was no longer needed as much to handle speaking engagements at churches since I could now share first-hand about the needs in Ukraine. We tried to limit travel to two weekends per month, especially since we had become heavily involved at Community Christian. Time management stresses reached almost unbearable levels, and we knew it would be impossible to continue 80-85 hour workweeks indefinitely.

Funds that had been donated and held by MASTER Provisions were not yet sufficient to meet our family needs in early 1996. Dan encouraged me to become an official part of the staff of Community. The church leadership team worked out a salary offer in order that I could be paid as a part-time minister beginning in May. (Tanya still would not be married to a full-time preacher so that part of the deal remained barely intact.) WOW! This was the last piece of the puzzle: full-time with MP and part-time at Community! In actuality, the pay was part-time, but the work was full-time. At least I would not have three full-time jobs if I left Cincy Bell.

I am very grateful to Dan for his willingness to take a risk by asking a "lay" person to become his associate pastor. He also challenged me regularly in the areas of personal spiritual growth. The practice of reading a Psalm a day (repeating Psalms every five months), reading a Proverb a day (repeating Proverbs each month) and reading from the Old Testament and New Testament each day (reading the entire Bible each year) became a habit. Spiritual strength acquired from time with the Lord first thing each morning enabled me to survive the rigorous daily schedule.

Surely any remaining doubts in my mind about moving into full-time missions work would be washed away if I took one more trip to Ukraine. I planned an April excursion to Ukraine with Jim

Smelser and Jon Guess to check on the clothing ministry one more time. MP intrigued Jim when we first started, and he wanted to join me on the trip along with Jon. Jon, a manager at Norfolk & Southern Railroad, provided free rail transportation on container shipments from Cincinnati or Louisville to the port at Norfolk. What a huge blessing to MASTER Provisions as we nickeled and dimed our way to growth by God's grace extended through people like Jon.

It was actually very interesting how the relationship with Norfolk & Southern evolved through our good friend, Byron Ford. Byron worshipped with us at First Church of Christ back in the 80's prior to being transferred out of town. He and his wife, Sandy, visited First Church in June 1994 for the first time in many years. They were not sure why, but Byron felt compelled to visit. The first clothing drive in MP history kicked off that very Sunday. Byron was moved by Joe's stirring stories about hardships in the inflation-ravaged former Soviet Union country. After the service, he asked us how we planned to transport the loads of clothing overseas. I shared that we were evaluating shipping containers by truck, rail and ship to Ukraine. Byron's company takes care of the railroad portion of the transportation process. That next week, Byron approached Norfolk & Southern management with the idea of helping MASTER Provisions with free railroad transportation from Louisville to Norfolk, Virginia. Byron did all of the legwork and received eventual corporate approval through Jon Guess to assist MASTER Provisions. Norfolk & Southern helped us in this manner for over four years and saved thousands of "Kingdom dollars" for MP.

Off we flew to Ukraine to see if my heart convictions would turn into head decisions. Sure enough, incidents occurred daily during the trip that brought closure in my mind regarding secular employment. I knew that MASTER Provisions was my calling in life. Jon, Jim and I enjoyed many of the same experiences that thrilled my soul a year earlier. What a glorious experience it is to share your life, Christ and clothing with physically needy and spiritually inquiring people!

We returned in the middle of April, and the first day back at Cincinnati Bell was one of the most anticipated days of my life. That was the day when I would schedule a meeting with upper management to discuss my career intentions. The Friday after returning to work, the District Manager met with me. After sharing about the trip, I told him that I would be leaving Cincinnati Bell in two weeks to serve in full-time Christian mission work. Although relatively shocked by the news, he understood and actually respected my decision.

Now, if you think I had the smile that could never be erased after returning from my first mission trip in 1995, nothing could compare with the smile on my face that extended from my heart. Finally, I was totally obedient to God's call for my life. The workplace gossip mills buzzed with activity about the decision and almost everyone was truly excited for my future — a future following a call that was no longer against my will!

My last day on the job to end a 17-year career in telecommunications fell on May 3, 1996. Ordination Sunday followed at Community Christian, on Sunday, May 5. The elders at CCC formally set me apart for full-time Christian service. People from the past surprised me and said all manner of kind things about me, truthful or other-

**I made a commitment to God: There would be no turning back to secular employment!**

wise. It was a wonderful family celebration and a day forever etched in the archives of my brain. Relatives and family members joined us on that special day. *I made a commitment to God: There would be no turning back to secular employment!* Doubts had been divinely erased, and a new era in Life Babik had begun with great excitement and expectation!

CHAPTER *6*

# Post-Obedience Blessings

Did you ever think about what would happen if God show-ered blessings on us just because we "thought about" doing what He wanted us to do? Of course, there would be very little follow through in matters requiring faith. The Biblical pattern is always the same: God's blessings come after one chooses to obey. *God expects doing, not thinking about doing.* He demands a faith accompanied by obedience.

Consider Abraham. Abraham was doing pretty well in life, but it was not until he left the land he loved and everything he knew that God opened the floodgates of heaven's blessings. How about Joseph? He honored God's mandate for sexual purity and did not cave in to Mrs. Potiphar's advances. As a result, Joseph eventually became quite a royal consultant, specializing in

**God expects doing, not thinking about doing.**

55

dream interpretation. The end result of his journey in captivity, and God's sovereign blessing, was management of the largest stockpile of riches in the world at that time. Job had more than his share of hard knocks, but he refused to curse God. His obedience unto the death of everyone he loved, except his wife, led Job to the title of World's Wealthiest "Woe-Sufferer". However, his post-obedience blessings more than doubled his net worth, and he truly enjoyed the golden years because he obeyed God.

I'm not here to tell you that a financial windfall rolled our way after obeying God's call to trust Him by entering full-time vocational Christian service. That would be false. In fact, our income was cut by more than 50%, and we lost CBT's lucrative health-care and savings packages. But, I will share the fact that God blessed us abundantly after I chose to obey Him fully. The blessings were a direct result of friends who cared and just wanted to say: "I love you" in different ways. *God likes to use His people to bless His people.* So, let's count some of God's post-obedience blessings.

**ONE:** Less than a month after "the decision", a wonderful doctor from church, Doc Charles Caldwell, learned of our commitment to missions and offered his services to us at no charge. A couple of years later, another Christian doctor friend, Greg Koo, made the same generous offer, which helped our family for numerous years. In addition, whenever available, both doctors gave us office samples of pharmaceuticals to save on drug charges. So, our family has been blessed with real God-Class Physician Care and Prescription Drug Programs. The world

**God likes to use His people to bless His people.**

looks at modest co-payment fees for office visits as a good deal, but God used a couple of His medical practitioners to give us free services. That's certainly a divine health care plan.

**TWO:** One of our first financial supporters is a dear friend who improves smiles. When he heard of "the decision", he told us that if any of the young ones ever needed orthodontic care, we could consider those treatments a gift to our ministry and family. Three out of the four young Babiks ended up receiving dental alignments. Indeed, we were tremendously blessed to receive this complimentary care from a devoted Christian orthodontist, Dr. Tim Perkins.

**THREE:** God is really good at details, and He knew that dental care is fairly expensive, too. So, He led a God-fearing family dentist, Dr. Joe Brown, to crown us with many crowns or to fill unwanted holes in our pearly whites or just do routine cleanings and check-ups. In addition, Dr. Brown made a sacrificial financial gift to establish a dental clinic in Ukraine. He invested one summer vacation and brought several assistants with him to assist hundreds of needy people on behalf of MASTER Provisions at the dental clinic he helped to establish in Kakhovka, Ukraine.

**FOUR:** Lifting lots of clothes bags weighing over 80 pounds and assuming near-contortionist positions in order to load clothing containers takes a toll on the human body. I had never thought about the benefits of chiropractic care. Chiropractors are the experts who align spines and melt all of those subluxations away. Yes, I learned everything you never knew about subluxations; that is, nerve interference in the spinal cord that leads to physical impairment and disease. A wonderful Christian chiropractor, Dr. Paul Bryngelson, offered to treat our active family as needed and has helped out for many years. Complimentary

"Crack-the-back-ter" care: just another in the line of God's physical blessings for the Babiks!

**FIVE:** Within the first two years, over thirty individuals and churches lined up to offer financial gifts from which our monthly salary and other ministry expenses could be paid. We certainly operated on a faith-only basis in regards to pay day, and many churches and friends were found faithful. Not once in the first ten years of full-time service with MASTER Provisions were there insufficient funds to pay our monthly salary established by the Board of Directors.

**SIX:** The blessing of cross-cultural friendships is invaluable. Thanks to electronic mail and drastically reduced phone rates, it's even easy to keep in touch regularly these days. You find a common thread amongst believers in Christ who live in economically distressed countries. They have great joy and peace that is not in any way related to physical comfort or riches. They understand the true treasure of well-invested time with loved ones. You see people who make time to share their time with others all the time! You enjoy worship services not confined to one hour. You learn to share your faith with others on a daily basis. And, you discover how to pray about everything. Yes, believers in impoverished countries put a face on the challenge found in Philippians 4:6-7: "Do not be anxious about anything but in EVERYTHING, by prayer and petition, with thanksgiving, present your requests to God. And the peace of God, which transcends all understanding, will guard your hearts and minds in Christ Jesus." (emphasis mine).

You learn a lot about the Christian life from believers overseas. Oleg Shishkin, pastor of a Christian church in Kakhovka, Ukraine, is a man of God's power, peace and prayer. Oleg turns every single thing over to God in prayer. During a summer mission trip, one of our team workers, Anne Wise, accidentally butted heads with a Ukrainian teen during a game. She became dizzy and nauseous for a couple of days and was subject to fainting. One of our team members, who was an RN, suggested that Anne was displaying signs of a spinal cord injury. The American concept of immediate medical evacuation was challenged by Oleg's call to obeying God's Word in prayer. Oleg referred to the passage in James 5:13-16 where we are commanded to anoint with oil and pray in faith for God to make the sick person well. Oleg asked Anne, who was feeling very ill, if she believed that God could heal her. Anne said, "Yes," and so an elder, Oleg and I gathered to pray with Anne. After a long time of prayer, confession of sins and praise, Oleg anointed Anne's head with oil, and we laid hands on her and prayed. As we prayed in faith, I felt Anne's head trembling and getting hot. As we finished praying, it was as if Anne had snapped out of a semi-comatose state. After the prayer, she told us that the dizziness and nausea left immediately and she felt fine again. Anne said she experienced tremendous warmth as we prayed. The pain was gone! God had healed her, just as He promises in His Word. People of faith around the world sharpen us and strengthen our faith.

**SEVEN:** Being absolutely convinced, beyond the shadow of any doubt, that you are doing what God made you to do brings incredible joy and satisfaction. *In general terms, for EVERY Christian, our purpose is to take on Christ's purpose.* What

**In general terms, for EVERY Christian, our purpose is to take on Christ's purpose.**

was Jesus' purpose? Jesus Christ clearly stated his own purpose in Luke 19:10: "For the Son of Man came to seek and to save what was lost." So, each of us needs to be involved in our Heavenly Father's business of looking for and saving people who are lost; people who are living outside of a relationship with Jesus Christ. Regardless of vocational calling, all Christians should adopt that purpose for living. It's just doubly, triply, maybe even "quadruply" satisfying when even your daily vocation consists of doing that which accomplishes Christ's purpose of seeking and saving the lost. Christian vocational employment maximizes opportunities to be used to seek and save the lost and provides eternal job satisfaction.

**EIGHT:** Mission ministries like MASTER Provisions are totally dependent for success and growth on a huge volunteer network. Interaction with volunteers yields mutual fun and encouragement. It's a blast to work side by side with people of all ages and skills. It is very gratifying to see others catch a vision for missions through involvement in a clothing drive here or by serving on our mission teams abroad. Volunteers brighten your days, weeks and months and are the literal lifeline for missions work. Over 4,000 people volunteer each year to help sort, pack and load clothing or to work with us on mission trips in places like Honduras, India, Kosova and Ukraine.

This seemingly unending flow of God's blessings has been available for our enjoyment since the day I finally decided to

**The initial fears and doubts associated with leaving behind the "security" of corporate life were washed away completely in the shower of God's goodness.**

follow God in total obedience. There is no doubt that I would have lost out on this incredible source of joy and encouragement had I continued in stubborn rejection of God's higher call against my will. *The initial fears and doubts associated with leaving behind the "security" of corporate life were washed away completely in the shower of God's goodness.* There has never been one day, not even one moment, when I looked back with regret at following God's divine plan for my life. Praise God from whom all post-obedience blessings flow!

# CHAPTER 7

# Tests Over Time

Yes, the blessings were evident and doubts had been erased. Although there were never moments of "Lot's Wife's Longings and Looking Back", there were plenty of tests over time. Isn't life really a series of tests for all of us? And, passing one test never means that the next test will be any easier.

James knew all about this testing business. He explained in the first chapter of his letter to the twelve scattered tribes that life's tests are not about gaining knowledge. They are about growing in faith, which develops perseverance and leads to maturity and completeness. *God allows tests during life to get us to the point where we do not lack anything needed to live in undivided devotion to Him.*

**God allows tests during life to get us to the point where we do not lack anything needed to live in undivided devotion to Him.**

Let's simply classify our family and ministry tests into three categories: spiritual, natural and physical.

## Spiritual Test #1: GREED REVEALED

Clothing operations began with predictable slowness in Ukraine in 1994. We learned the hard way that it is very difficult to start any new venture in a post-Communist culture. Fear had gripped the lives of people, and very few Ukrainians were willing to make decisions. Joe selected one of the few capable leaders recommended by the church in Kherson to serve as the first director of the clothing ministry. Kostia, a former ship captain, accustomed to making quick decisions, also served as a pastor and was well respected in the church and community. Therefore, Kostia was charged with the responsibility to hire the first workers and to make all other business decisions. He enabled us to establish all of the operating procedures and interfaced with Ukrainian customs officials to create all necessary documents and forms.

Kostia not only helped us to negotiate in "customs-land", he also helped to navigate the uncharted territories of business dealings with Joe's fledgling farming operations. He was given much authority and responsibility. Kostia was able to get the first warehouse and clothes shops opened with minimal delays, and he hired the first six workers at Blagodat. Blagodat is the Russian word meaning "grace". The Blagodat clothing shop opened in the fourth quarter of 1994. Everything seemed to be going well initially until we learned of various problems within the church as a result of the clothing ministry. After investigating these reports, we soon discovered that Kostia and the store manager had been taking some of the best clothing and selling it for personal profit.

Kostia and the dishonest manager were fired, a series of meetings with field missionaries and church leaders were conducted, and it was decided to continue the ministry with more stringent accountability standards between Blagodat and the church leaders. The outreach of MP nearly ended within its first year as a result of a "Judas" in the ranks. Praise God! The storm was weathered, and our Heavenly Father provided new leadership that was not tempted by the greed monster.

## Spiritual Test #2: PRIDE REPEALED

When any task, project or ministry is successful, you must be wary of a monster that likes to rear its ugly head for all to see. *That mischievous and unwanted intruder is an enemy called pride.* Satan is the inventor and master of pride, and he eternally lost his relationship with God because of it. He fell from a lofty position of ministry for God due to pride. Pride can be simply defined as taking personal credit for anything instead of giving all glory, thanks and praise to God for everything.

It is so easy for pride to innocently sneak onto the scene, even in mission work. Pride blurts out garbage like "my ministry" or "my mission trip" instead of a proper and humble "God's ministry" or "God's mission trip". MASTER Provisions was God's baby from the start. Why, I did not even want to follow God's call to ministry initially! But, once things got rolling and MP was successful, it was easy for feelings of pride to overshadow the proper and humble response of gratitude to God at all times for all things.

**That mischievous and unwanted intruder is an enemy called pride.**

When pride creeps in, be sure that God will do what it takes to clean up a proud heart. We either humble ourselves in God's sight, or He will make sure that we are humbled. After three years of growth and one wonderful year of full-time service at MP, God used our first large-team mission trip, in the summer of 1997, to remind me who was in charge of MASTER Provisions. MP was not my ministry nor did I lead my mission trips.

My "great" idea about working to refurbish the Kherson Christian Church building fizzled and led to frustrations for everyone involved. In addition, one of the team members wanted to operate independently from the rest of the group. We experienced conflict because I viewed his actions as interfering with my plans instead of possibly complicating God's plans. He preferred to take an interpreter and chart his own activity course. I learned the hard way that I needed to be flexible on mission trips and allow others room to deviate from my plans. During the trip home, I realized that my ego, plans and pride could hinder God's higher plans. I asked God to forgive me and peel away the pride that harms ministry. In addition, I committed to being flexible in every aspect of ministry leadership rather than be a proud, control freak. *When we give God a chance to be God in all circumstances, everything always works out so nicely.*

### Natural Test #1: UNDERGROUND UNDERWATER WAREHOUSE.

Our initial donated warehouse space consisted of 2,000 square feet in the center of the Boone-Kenton warehouse in

. . . . . . . . . . . . . . . . . . . . . . . . . . . . . . . . . . . . . . . . . .

**When we give God a chance to be God in all circumstances, everything always works out so nicely.**

. . . . . . . . . . . . . . . . . . . . . . . . . . . . . . . . . . . . . . . . . .

Florence, Kentucky. Owner Shirley Elliot was so incredibly gracious to give us this space at no charge for seven years. However, the warehouse was not heated, and it was sometimes difficult to recruit volunteers to sort and pack clothing during the frigid winter months. It wasn't long before a friend at church with a dry cleaning business very close to the warehouse said we could use heated space in the basement of her facility. It was so nice to have a warm place to work from November through March, even though it was a bit of a struggle to haul clothing up and down the staircase. After all, we only worked there occasionally, and at least we could stay warm. During the second winter of using the basement facility, a water line sprung a leak in the basement. It took a while to notice the problem, and, by that time, a bunch of clothing sitting on the basement floor was mildew infested. Fortunately, it was only the bottom layer of clothing that was ruined. Some good friends at Community Christian pitched in to help clean up the smelly mess, and we carted ruined clothing off to a dumpster. The Lord seemed to be teaching us that comfort is not always in our best interest.

## Natural Test #2: ROOF RAISING

In the summer of 2000, a mini-tornado classified as a microburst ripped through Florence and tore the roof off our home at the Boone-Kenton warehouse. Unfortunately, it was the section of the warehouse against the west wall of the building where our clothing pile resided that received the brunt of the damage. Torrential rains followed the microburst and soaked tons of clothing. Mr. Elliot called to let us know about the catastrophe. Again, an incredible outpouring of volunteer assistance from our friends at Community saved the day. Some ran load after load of laundry, dried the clothes and returned them to the warehouse. Others took truckloads of wet clothing to nearby laundromats. Many hands helped to dry off "ready-to-ship" bags of clothing. We only lost a small amount of clothing due to the quick response of friends.

The state fire marshals examined the warehouse following the storm. In their concluding report, they indicated that our operation at the warehouse constituted a fire hazard. The fire patrollers told Shirley Elliot, the owner, that he would need to install a sprinkler system in the warehouse in order to allow us to stay. The proposed, exorbitant expense made no business sense, so Shirley was forced to ask us to leave the warehouse against his wishes. He seemed broken-hearted as he informed us about this decision, but it would be nearly two years before we understood why God had allowed this mishap.

A late Saturday evening in February 2002 found me in Richmond, Virginia, where I was scheduled to speak on behalf of MP that next morning. The phone rang about 10:00 p.m. and it was Tanya. I figured she was checking on my safe arrival, but she actually called to report that there had been a different kind of burst at our old home, the Boone-Kenton warehouse. A massive fire, that made national news, ignited suddenly that evening and the entire building burst into flames and was completely destroyed in short order. If we had still been at the warehouse, MP would have lost 2½ containers worth of clothing that was already sorted and packed and awaiting shipment in March and April. This was certainly one time where a major hassle (water clean up after the microburst) was God's hand at work in advance to protect us. We learned not to get upset when circumstances seem difficult or unfair. Look for God at work in such times!

## Physical Test #1: CELL MALFUNCTION

Summer 2003 was overloaded as usual with activities like kids' camps, ball games and mission trips. Even the hacking cough that surfaced for Tanya in August was normal because that's about the time each year when fall allergies flare up. The night sweats that surfaced on fall nights were slightly unexpected but no big surprise since we had heard that they often accompany the onset of menopause. After all, Tanya's mom had undergone every woman's favorite stage of life beginning in her forties. And the gradual loss in weight was actually welcomed a bit as it is for all middle-agers, right? Surely, the itchiness and rash had to do with the change to a different fabric softener. We simply stopped using the new brand and went back to our first choice in softeners. The switch back to the original product would help to clear up the itching, but it would not happen immediately, you know. The holidays rolled around and chocolates just did not have the same taste appeal to Tanya, an admitted chocolate addict. That seemed strange, but it's good not to eat sweets anyway at that time of year when it is so easy to gain weight. Actually, it was the first time she ever remembered losing weight during the holidays.

I started to put together the pieces as Tanya's weight continued to drop and her appetite and energy levels decreased. She was able to fit into clothes passed down by our youngest daughter, Joy, and was finally back to her desired wedding weight. By late November, I told Tanya that she should set a doctor's appointment to see what was going on inside of her. However, with seasonal festivities fast approaching and all of the busyness at that time of year, Tanya thought it would be best to wait until after the holidays.

## Physical Test #2: CAR MALFUNCTION

MP's staff Christmas party was set for Saturday, December 13 at Dave Mayer and Don Davisson's shared farmhouse in Harrison County. Good old Saturday the 13th! Only Joy, Tanya and I were able to attend, so we headed south about 4:30 that afternoon. The temperature was below freezing, and a light snow was falling. We considered canceling the party, but that would not be good, surely. Then we discussed which car to drive; the Sable with front-wheel drive that handles better on slippery roads or the old 1988 Volvo that is built like a tank. We decided to go with the Volvo for no apparent reason.

Less than 15 miles down the interstate, just as the passenger side seat-warmer reached a cozy temperature, the mix of frigid temperature, strong winds and snow caused black ice to form on the highway in a construction area. We hit the black stuff traveling 60 miles per hour and immediately the car began swaying out of control. What a weird feeling! It felt like we were hydroplaning down a river. Perhaps it would have been thrilling had we donned crash helmets and armor suits with no other cars on the highway, but the interstate was crowded with holiday traffic and we were not physically prepared for the adventure. The calmly spoken words, "God help us", were uttered, because I realized He was the only One that could get us out of this mess. We smashed into a concrete abutment on the passenger side, and the impact caused the hood to fly up as the front right side of the car caved in and the tire blew. We barely slowed down, and I slid down in my seat to try to see what was going on through the small slat between the dash and the bottom of the raised hood. Boom! We smacked the abutment in the center, as we careened like a pinball down I-75. "God save us!" I cried urgently, as we headed out of control off the highway to the right. At that moment, we felt a huge thud against the passenger side of the car that caved in both doors next to Tanya and Joy. I glanced over to see a God-inspired driver in a Cadillac Escalade who had come along beside us to absorb quite an initial jolt. Then, he turned into us with a second, less violent blow from his left fender to our already crushed right front side. Amazingly, he used his brand new vehicle like a stock car to end our skid and drag us off to the side of the highway. To our astonishment as we looked at his car, there was not even a scratch or dent on the side of the Escalade that slammed into the Volvo with sufficient force to cave in both doors. Only a minor dent on the front fender yielded a hint of the divine feat that had been accomplished. Perhaps a couple of angels needed wing replacement surgery, but the Cadillac was in great shape!

We thanked the Lord and stepped out of the totaled vehicle just as another car flipped on its top on the center divider and then landed about eight feet from us in the center lane facing oncoming traffic. An 18-wheeler miraculously stopped a few feet from the lady driver whose pupils seemed silver dollar sized as she prepared for the worst in those precious seconds.

All of the traffic had finally come to a standstill behind us. Our accident literally blocked the interstate as steam rolled out from the Volvo's radiator. During the following minutes as we comforted the female driver and awaited the ambulance, we enjoyed some interesting conversations. The big rig driver plainly stated that only God could have allowed him to stop and not run over the lady who had wrecked right in front of him. The driver of the Escalade was a retired police officer. He frankly was not sure how he reacted so quickly to perhaps save our lives. However, I believe that God answered our desperate cry to save us by putting the right person in the right place with the right vehicle and right disposition and the right experience to save us. We thanked God for His deliverance! The car was history, the trunk looked like it had suffered an atomic green bean casserole explosion, our youngest daughter had a stress headache from the "Joy-ride", the Christmas party was cancelled, but no one perished. God showed His ability to deliver us from death's door!

## Physical Test #1: CELL MALFUNCTION (Continued)

During the weeks after the wreck, Tanya noticed a lot of soreness and discomfort in the middle of her chest. That had to be pain from where the seatbelt jerked across her chest. There was even a little bump and red spot that had formed and would not go away. Surely, that was a bruise and irritation resulting from the car wreck.

After Christmas, Tanya received some fairly urgent reminders that her condition was not getting better and she needed to get a medical examination. In spite of drenching night sweats, weight loss, loss of appetite, general fatigue, no desire for chocolates or any other life pleasures, itchiness, hives and a red spot and discomfort in the middle of her chest, she grudgingly agreed to start blood tests in January. When various blood tests turned up negative, our family doctor ordered chest X-rays in February just before Tanya accompanied Lydia to Florida for a national cheerleading competition. When he saw the X-rays, *Doc Koo knew there was something rotten under the "chest mark"*. The

. . . . . . . . . . . . . . . . . . . . . . . . . . . . . . . . . . . .
**Doc Koo knew there was something rotten under the "chest mark".**
. . . . . . . . . . . . . . . . . . . . . . . . . . . . . . . . . . . .

X-ray showed a large mass in the middle of her chest. He did not want to call Tanya with the bad news in Florida and waited until the day she returned. CT-scans were performed on the following Wednesday. The next morning was one that would be forever etched into our minds.

Rocket science degrees are not needed for anyone to know that an 8 a.m. phone call from your doctor asking to see you and your spouse immediately isn't a call to inform you that all is well health-wise. That call came on Thursday morning, February 19, 2004. Tanya and I arrived at the doctor's office at 12:30. Doctor Koo began crying. He is more than a doctor; he is a close personal friend. I said that we needed to pray. We already knew what he was going to tell us. The oncology office had called Tanya in mid-morning to schedule a 1:45 appointment. After leading a prayer for God's strength to get through the situation and asking that He be glorified in this and all circumstances, we learned officially that Tanya had cell malfunction and we would be referred to a cancer doctor.

The oncologist, who had also treated my dad, explained the plan of action that required a biopsy in order to determine the exact type of cancer. Even though the situation was certainly not good, it is not wise to start a course of treatment before identifying the actual type of cancer.

The three weeks between cancer notification day and B-day (biopsy day) were filled with many visits from dear friends and acts of service such as helping Tanya paint the basement. Her husband had put the project off long enough, and he was in Florida for a MASTER Provisions work project. We were blessed when a large group of great friends completed work in one day, which would have taken us weeks to accomplish.

On the Sunday morning immediately preceding the biopsy, God awakened me early with a series of comforting thoughts. He clearly told me that the cancer in Tanya's life would be used to strengthen my faith and witness for Him. God gave me the distinct instruction not to worry and He would take care of Tanya. So, I determined to hold on to God's words, no matter what circumstances arose. Our Lord gave me the strength to carry on and remain positive and confident that the outcome was under His sovereign control.

We reported to St. Elizabeth Hospital in Edgewood, Kentucky, at 5:30 a.m. on March 11. One of our friends and a co-parent from Ryle High School is a nurse for the heart surgeon who was called on to perform the biopsy. Her presence as well as her confidence in the doctor was very reassuring. All signs pointed to lymphoma, but taking a slice of the tumor was required for accurate cell deformation analysis. Paula, my sister-in-law, and Sybille Raymond, a friend from church, sat beside me stoically in the St. E waiting room and offered listening ears and hearts. The procedure started about 8:00 a.m., and the doctor called me into a conference room two hours later after they had examined the tissue sample. I was my usual lighthearted self and asked the doctor if he was able to find anything wrong, but doc was all business. With little ado, he said, "Mr. Babik, I have some bad news. Your wife has lung cancer, Stage 4, and she, most likely, has 6-12 months to live." Rather than reel at the news, I responded that everything would work out and Tanya would be OK. The doctor simply shook his head and said, "You do not understand the seriousness of this situation. The main tumor is large, one lung is collapsed and the cancer has already metastasized to three other spots." I thanked the doctor for his work and replied, "Doc, we serve a great God. Tanya will be fine." He shook his head again as I returned to the waiting room.

Paula and Sibylle eagerly awaited the news. I shared the doctor's sobering prognosis and told them that we had to go by faith here and not by what we had been told. We prayed to that end and were comforted by God's presence. We had sent the Babik kids to school that day, and I began to think of the best way to let them know the not-so-pleasant news du jour.

James tells us to ask God when we discover a wisdom shortage. There's a daily shortfall of that for me anyway, and this day I really needed God's wisdom to show me how to break the news to my children. God was faithful as always. He led me to the account in John, Chapter 9, where Jesus miraculously healed the man born blind. The Lord counseled me to read the first 11 verses of that story and substitute Tanya and cancer for the man and blindness. Our four children and I gathered around Tanya's hospital bed that night. We prayed expectantly. Then, I began to read the divinely inspired paraphrase of John 9:1-3 and 6-11. "As Jesus went along, He saw a lady named Tanya, who had been stricken with lung cancer at age 45. The Babik children asked him, 'Rabbi, who sinned, our Mom or her parents, that she should have this cancer?' 'Neither your Mom nor her parents sinned,' said Jesus, 'but this happened so that the work of God might be displayed in her life.' Having said this, Jesus comforted Tanya and laid His healing hand upon her. 'Go,' He told her, 'and I will wash away your cancer.' So, Tanya was healed and the cancer was gone.' Tanya's neighbors and those who had seen her sick with a deadly cancer asked, 'Isn't this the lady who had gotten very weak and was dying of cancer?' Some claimed that she was. Others said, 'No, it only looks like her.' But Tanya herself insisted, 'I am the woman!' 'How can the cancer be removed?' they demanded. She replied, 'The man they call Jesus told me to have faith and the cancer would be washed away. So, I put my faith in Him, and the cancer was removed.'"

In an emotional chat, I told the kids about the vision God gave me not to worry about Mom, and everything would be fine. We had to all hold onto the faith that God could heal her. Regardless of what we could see or what we were told, we must hold onto faith in God, our Great Physician. We needed to be very careful about what we said, so that we would not unintentionally undermine the power of God at work around us. We felt the prayers of many people giving us strength. All four teenaged children displayed remarkable faith and maturity. There was zero evidence of any fear in the room.

Mark and Pam Scherer entered the room shortly after we enjoyed this wonderful time of sharing from God's Word. Pam is a woman devoted to prayer, and she sees visions from God. As she had been praying about Tanya's health status the night before, God spoke to her in a vision, which she shared with all of us. In the vision, Tanya was sitting on a park bench, tired and worn out. Angels surrounded her and ministered to her for a short time. Then, Roger and Tanya were soon dancing together and praising God with great joy. Pam said she did not have an interpretation, but she wanted to share that vision. As we chatted and put together God's assuring words to me with God's comforting vision given to Pam, I told everyone that the interpretation seemed obvious to me. Tanya would go through this time of great sickness, feeling weak and alone. God would minister to her and in a short time, she would be restored to health. There would be great joy at the Babik house, because God would heal her.

That evening sapped our emotions. We started a prayer chain that literally spread around the world overnight. People reported spending all night in prayer and others entered a time of fasting. Tanya slept restlessly that night, and a teary-eyed Doctor Koo joined us the next morning to review the results of the biopsy. I shared that Tanya was in God's good hands, and we must not lose faith in what God would be able to do.

The first dramatic change in Tanya's status occurred in late afternoon. The oncologist was in an obviously jubilant mood, as he shared that it now looked like the cell make-up pointed to Non-Hodgkin's Lymphoma instead of Lung Cancer. They had no explanation for the change in diagnosis, and some believe that God changed the cancer in response to the prayers of many righteous saints around the world. I did not know. It did not matter. I was operating under divine mandate to hold onto God's assurance of healing regardless of what anyone said. The change in prognosis sounded promising, and Tanya was released from the hospital on Saturday morning.

The oncologist indicated that the cancer was advanced and had already spread inside Tanya's abdomen. The large tumor in the middle of Tanya's chest that caused the collapsed lung and pneumonia concerned the medical staff. According to their best judgments, there were no guarantees of success, but an intensive course of chemotherapy and radiation might help to battle the cancer. I was convinced that God works both within and outside the confines of modern medicine, so the decision about treatment was left up to Tanya. The following Tuesday became Chemo Day #1, when cancer-killing drugs were intravenously injected into her bloodstream during a grueling, six-hour session.

Hair loss was the greatest woe during the entire bout with cancer. However, Tanya's faith was exemplary. She told everyone that she wanted whatever would be best for God to be done for her. King James would record her desire as: "May whatever is best for Thee be done to Thy servant." So, if her healing and recovery would be to God's ultimate advantage, so be it. If heavenly relocation was best, then may all people say, "AMEN." We differed on this view about her recovery, because I was convinced that God would heal her and be glorified in that manner. Sometimes I wondered if I was walking by faith or just by hope of what I wanted to happen, but I had to hold onto the thoughts God implanted back in February. Little emaciated, bald Tanya blessed many during the three months of chemotherapy.

The one word that stuck out on the one-month, post-diagnosis report was "remarkable". The incredible shrinking tumor and associated spots amazed the doctors. The second and third month analyses used that same "r" word. In accordance with Pam's vision and God's healing mercy, the cancer remarkably achieved "total remission status". Less than five months after I had heard the "6 to 12 months to live" speech, the unwelcome guest no longer resided in Tanya's earthly tent. Diffuse large-cell non-Hodgkin's lymphoma was completely gone! Praise God!

*Part* 3
# Blessed in His Will

# CHAPTER 8

# *Storehouse Gifts*

Great growth of any mission thrives on God's grace extended through generous givers! Jesus told us it is more blessed to give than to receive, but He certainly did not say it was not a blessing to receive. From its inception, MP has been incredibly blessed through gifts made of plastic, cardboard, wheels and walls. Such gifts represent thousands of dollars of gift-in-kind donations over the years to the MASTER Provisions storehouse.

## PLASTIC GIFTS

As we started to collect donated clothing in 1994 while I still worked at Cincinnati Bell, we immediately recognized the need for adequate packing and storing methods. Using plastic bags provided by Kenny Hicks, we experimented by stuffing clothing down into every square inch of the bags. They seemed to work just fine, from the very first bag packed in Joe Parker's garage. The fine art of clothes cramming had begun, much to the chagrin of the average female. Ladies, you know, carefully fold each piece of donated clothing only to see savages jam the previously unwrinkled garment into a nook or cranny of available air space. The bag-packing method certainly points to the fact that MP is a male-run clothing ministry. We quickly learned to double up the bags, since they were apt to explode on the seam when excess pressure was applied. After all, they probably were not designed to hold 80 pounds of clothing. The most difficult part was hand-tying knots to close the top of the 40-inch tall bags. Those weak office hands and forearms cramped up for the first couple of months until they got used to the stress. Each week, Kenny was faithful in collecting one company's trash that turned into our clothes-packing treasures.

In the early 2000's, our good friend Bill Heaton, Associate Pastor at Berean Baptist Church in Mansfield, Ohio, introduced me to David Frecka, owner of Next Generation Films in nearby Lexington. We showed Dave the bags we had used for packing for nearly 10 years and explained that they frequently burst because they were fairly rigid. The size was perfect but the flexibility was not. A true plastics manufacturing guru, Dave tugged, bit and tore the bag and then designed the exact bags that we now use for clothes packing. Same size, just tougher and more pliable, and we no longer would have to double up the bags. Next Generation Films now donates thousands of dollars worth of custom-manu-factured "clothes-packing" bags each year to MP.

## CARDBOARD GIFTS

Each shipment of clothing to an economically distressed country consists of approximately 90 percent clothing and 10 per-cent footwear and accessories. Instead of bagging the non-clothing items, we send them in cardboard boxes. For the first seven years, we scrounged around for any boxes that could be found to use for packing footwear. Loading the non-standard boxes into a container was always a challenge akin to working a jigsaw puzzle with missing pieces. It was always time consuming and frustrating, and wasted space was the norm.

Jim Smelser was leading a clothes and shoe-packing event at a church in Kentucky and noticed that someone had donated items in some very sturdy boxes labeled Wood-Mizer. He thought how nice it would be to have such boxes for packing shoes and accessories but gave it little further thought. A couple of years later while sorting clothing at Chapel Rock Christian Church in Indianapolis, a lady named Phyllis Lazkowski was a volunteer that day. Jim found out that her husband, Don, was in charge of Wood-Mizer Products, Inc., a corporation headquartered in Indianapolis. Wood-Mizer is an outstanding company that believes in doing the right things for the right reasons. They manufacture portable sawmills and do lots of charitable work each year. Jim remembered the boxes he had seen in Kentucky and told Phyllis about the possible use of their boxes to transport shoes and accessories. Shortly thereafter, we received corporate approval from Wood-Mizer Products to use their very sturdy boxes to ship shoes and accessories overseas. The Wood-Mizer boxes fit into the shipping containers as if they were made for our purposes. They fit exactly five across and six rows tall with just a few inches of space left at the top of the container. We receive a monthly allotment of boxes from the generous folks at Wood-Mizer. As of late 2006, their boxes have made appearances in thirteen countries on five continents bearing precious cargo of footwear, belts, purses and hats.

## GIFTS ON WHEELS

The Babik family was willing to make the colossal financial adjustment from a near 6-figure income including incredible savings and benefits programs at Cincinnati Bell to a salary of less than $40,000 with no benefits at MP. In 1996, our 12-year-old Subaru with 200,000 miles, two broken door handles and windows, a rumble in the engine, etc., needed to relocate to the automotive graveyard. We regularly prayed it would manage to rattle on for another month. Rather than jumping out in fear to finance some new wheels, we prayed in faith that God would meet our needs. Within the first month of asking for God's intervention, my parents graciously offered their used vehicle as a donation to MP. So, the 1991 Mercury Sable became the first presidential limousine. That set of wheels lasted eight years and required only minor repairs and routine maintenance service.

By 2004, the Sable began to experience the problems associated with high-mileage, aging vehicles. Some anonymous donors lined up to purchase a 2000 Olds Intrigue at a bargain-basement price to replace the Mercury. The MP staff arranged a surprise party to present the vehicle to me. Only one major problem arose. The date planned for the special gift presentation was the very day that we learned about Tanya's cancer: February 19, 2004. So, the gathering to present the car to us turned into a meeting to bathe Tanya and our entire family in much-needed prayer. After the time of prayer, I was coaxed to walk out to the garage. There sat a wonderful gift. The good used car reminded us of God's love expressed through caring friends. It was a bittersweet day, as we rejoiced over the lovely gift and yet grieved over the gravity of the C-monster that was ravaging Tanya's body.

Clothes hauling presented logistical challenges from the outset of MP. It actually took us ten years to figure out that old trucks and buses become expendable to businesses for a reason: they reach a point of mechanical futility. A donated 1971 box truck was case-in-point number one. We never did figure out the miles per gallon (or was it gallons per mile?) or quarts of oil per 100 miles it needed to navigate the local highways, but it survived less than 2,000 miles of use before succumbing to engine fatigue.

School buses seemed like a good option to give us the ability to haul youth work groups and clothing. We started with a red and white school bus from a church down in Central Kentucky. On the inaugural trip from its old home to Indiana, the radiator hose blew on a long uphill grade. Six hundred dollars later, it was ready for action again. We were able to get some use out of the bus, just enough for us to think that the blown transmission within six months was merely bad fortune. The second bus was a different color but had similar internal problems. Maintenance expenses exceeded usefulness to the ministry, but we still were not convinced that school systems upgrade buses every so often for a reason. Jim earned the nickname "Broken Bus" Smelser during this period of vehicular malfunction.

We actually had one memorable family trip in school bus #2. We decided to take the whole Babik clan on an excursion to Champaign, Illinois for a clothes-packing event. Since they were home schooled at that time and did not have the opportunity to ride off to classes in a bus, they really enjoyed traveling in one. The kids had set up a card table and chairs in the area where bench seats had been removed. Daddy Driver got a little confused in a construction area by a detour in Indianapolis that came upon him faster than expected. He found out that buses do not handle swerves like cars do. The little jerk on the steering wheel to the left nearly sent the bus tipping over to the right. It certainly felt like we were two-wheeling for a few seconds and instantly made me realize how careful you need to be when transporting precious cargo. Thank God, He kept us upright and we escaped catastrophe. A couple of the kids deemed it a pretty neat feeling, but Co-Pilot Mrs. Babik quickly nixed the idea of an encore performance.

Although bus #2 also lasted less than one year, we decided to actually invest $4,000 in bus #3, a manual transmission beauty sure to last for years. We even purchased $1,500 worth of new tires, so certain were we that the third time of bus ownership would be a charming experience. Less than six weeks after obtaining a title to the bus that did not smoke while running, we allowed a CDL driver to use it to transport a group of students to a Christian summer camp in Central Kentucky. Uh, oh! The last bus experience involving Kentucky was certainly short and sweet. On the way home from camp, a southbound driver fell asleep behind the wheel, crossed the median and rammed into the driver's side of the bus. The tremendous jolt nearly pushed the large MP vehicle into a ravine.  By God's grace, the very experienced and competent driver was able to limp the bus to a stop before it hurtled to certain disaster. The insurance company declared bus #3 a total loss. We fought for six months to receive a reasonable settlement for the last school bus in MP history.

After the school bus fiascos, we decided to rent modern trucks, as needed, to meet hauling needs when a van and open trailer were not sufficient. That philosophy lasted for several years until we were offered another freebie, a 1980's vintage box truck no longer needed by a business in Indiana. Dave Mayer, staff worker and mechanic, invested several weeks to rebuild the engine and transmission on the free vehicle that cost over $2,500 to get on the road. That truck worked fairly well, but nine months later it chose to self-destruct on the interstate without causing injury. Finally and forever, we decided that while most gifts are extremely valuable to the ministry and greatly appreciated, aged trucks and buses would be denied access to the MP gift portfolio.

## GIFTS WITH WALLS

Storage space instantly became a need as streams of clothing flooded in during the summer of 1994. The temporary solution of Joe's garage quickly yielded to Boone-Kenton warehouse in Florence. The former burley tobacco warehouse served as our primary warehouse space for six years. Owner Shirley Elliot was incredibly generous to MP and even trusted us with keys to the back door for 24-hour access. We experienced the joys of a true climate-controlled environment; that is, the temperature outside determined the climate inside the warehouse. We sweated a lot in summer and froze a lot in winter, but the 2,000 square feet of space with semi-trailer dock access allowed us to load over fifty containers from that single location!

God has used good friends from First Church of Christ to provide additional warehouse space over the years. Jim Maddux assisted us tremendously the first few winters by offering an oversized garage bay at his residence for our use. Jim and Linda's place was only a 10-minute drive from the Babik ranch, so it was very convenient during those hectic transitional days from corporate life into full-time service with MP. Jim's fridge was always open to us and stocked with cold soft drinks for workers. We hosted a lot of work groups at the Maddux "warehouse" and restocked the fridge regularly. The Maddux family displayed extreme hospitality for several years. My most humbling moment in bus driving came the day when I inadvertently left the rear door open as I backed up to the garage and creased Jim's gutter. Boy, talk about feeling stupid! I also did the same number on our garage gutter at home with the same school bus. It was obvious that my calling was not as a school bus driver, particularly while driving in reverse!

After vacating Jim's garage, Lois Beegle, owner of Superior Cleaners, provided complimentary basement space at her business near the Boone-Kenton warehouse. We worked a couple of winters in the heated confines during bitter cold days. It seemed much easier to attract volunteers with the lure of a heated workspace during the frigid winters.

The sovereignly controlled events that took place in the summer of 2000 forced us to evacuate Boone-Kenton Warehouse against the owner's wishes. We informed friends of MP that we needed a new home, and Brian Ruholt came to the rescue. He made a proposal to management at Marathon Ashland Petroleum (MAP) that MASTER Provisions be permitted to use space in their Covington, Kentucky, warehouse as a corporate humanitarian assistance project. The Marathon legal department approved this arrangement within two months. We moved into a cozy 800-square foot home at MAP in December 2000. The heated warehouse space and adjacent loading dock served the needs of MP for many years. Over forty containers were shipped from the premises of MAP in the first six years.

In 2003, we received 1,600 square feet of heated storage space in Cincinnati, courtesy of Arnold Caddell. Arnold's son, Chris, another First Church member, traveled with MP to Ukraine on a mission trip, fell in love with the people and became extremely involved as a volunteer with MP. Chris and his wife, Eleni, have invested countless hours to assist us over the years. Chris now sits on the MP Board of Directors. An incredible amount of complimentary gifts with walls have been given to MP over the years, primarily because of the love and concern of friends from First Church.

CHAPTER *9*

# *Twice-Dead Volunteer*

L oving people with a heart for mission work donate countless hours of labor to MASTER Provisions. MP could not collect, sort, pack and ship over a million pounds of good used clothing and shoes each year to economically distressed countries without their help. An entire volume could be devoted to the exploits of MP's helpers. However, we will share the dramatic life story of just one such person, our twice-dead volunteer.

He laid motionless in the middle of a Southern Indiana highway on a snowy late fall night, November 15, 1996, to be exact. An alert oncoming driver in a semi-tractor observed the situation and immediately blocked the highway with his big rig. He simply wanted to be like Jesus and lend assistance to a fellow human in obvious need. That truck driver/country Gospel songwriter named Larry quickly knelt down beside the hulk of a young man who was bleeding profusely, lying unconscious on the icy highway. The accident report filed later revealed that the pickup truck from which he had been thrown had flipped not once, not twice, but 12 different times. Impact marks left on the pavement testified to the violence of the accident. Following flip number 12, the young man was thrown 195 feet and landed head first on Highway 156. Larry wrapped his arms gently around the crash victim much like Jesus would wrap his arms around a hurting child. He struggled with all his might to move the severely injured youth into the warm cab. He certainly detected divine assistance as he hoisted over 200 pounds upward. Never mind that blood would get all over his coat and inside the cab. He felt compelled to help rescue a perishing young man and prayed urgently for God to intervene and keep him alive.

Thanks to mobile communications, Larry convinced the local authorities to request emergency air evacuation services. The semi-truck was hardly a suitable vehicle for transport to the nearest hospital in a life or death race vs. time. Within 30 minutes, a chopper landed at the scene. As they quickly unloaded the stretcher, they were surprised to see that the dying young man had been moved into the cab of the tractor. Larry, with the able assistance of our Loving Father, gently laid the bleeding body onto the gurney. Swiftly, he was transferred via the Air Care helicopter to University Hospital in Cincinnati, Ohio. Doctors there awaited the arrival of Jacob Riley Parker, age 21, Union, Kentucky. Blood alcohol levels were off the charts, several types of drugs in his system, suffering from traumatic brain injury and loss of blood, unconscious, chance of survival — slim to none. His parents needed to be notified immediately. They received the phone call dreaded by all parents of youthful motor vehicle operators in the middle of the night.

During 16 hours of emergency surgery, physicians removed part of the right side of his skull and brain. In all, 20% of his gray matter had to be removed due to the severe contusion and irreversible tissue damage. One hundred and twenty staples were required to re-fasten skin to skull. Desperately praying parents, friends and a special truck driver friend maintained a prayer vigil that night and into the next day. Twice during surgery, Jake was pronounced dead. *But, God heard and answered those prayers, reviving a corpse twice.*

Following surgery, doctors met with Mr. and Mrs. Parker, Richard and Linda, and shared the good news, bad news scenario. The obvious good news was the fact that Jake had survived the long surgery and was miraculously revived twice. The bad news was that their comatose son, Jake, would probably exist in a vegetative state for the rest of his life. For sure, he would never walk again even if he survived the critical post-surgery hours. They were told to expect the worst. Someone with injuries so severe would not live to drink, drug and drive another day.

Days slipped into weeks and Jake remained comatose for four months at University Hospital. Jake became a human pin cushion as tubes and intravenous needles were inserted in nearly every square inch of Jake's ravaged body, even between his toes and fingers. By mid-March, Jake's 6 foot 6 inch frame had withered to a mere 85 pounds. Hopes for survival remained bleak, but a faithful Mom, Linda, stayed beside her son daily. She implored God's assistance, mercy and healing for Jake. As she had prayed for her son faithfully even during his many years of rebellion,

. . . . . . . . . . . . . . . . . . . . . . . . . . . . . . . . . . . . . . . . .

**But, God heard and answered those prayers, reviving a corpse twice.**

. . . . . . . . . . . . . . . . . . . . . . . . . . . . . . . . . . . . . . . . .

Linda prayed that God would use all of life's circumstances to bring Jake into the saved relationship with Jesus Christ.

Jake recalls sensing the presence of loved ones, especially his twin sister, Sarah, even while resting in a coma. On nights when Jake struggled with restless sleep, his family did not sleep well either. The Parker family fought the battle together. The coma was really a blessing, just like the head injury became a gift to Jake over the years. There would have been no way to tolerate the excruciating pain associated with the brain injuries. The coma was God's way to allow Jake's body time for perfect rest and peace, if not healing.

As was her practice, Linda Parker sat beside Jake praying in mid-March, 1997, as her son began to stir. Linda was a Licensed Practical Nurse in addition to being a devoted mother. She willingly gave up her paid profession in order to be Jake's private caretaker. Jake fought to wake up as his mother glistened with hope. As he came out of the coma, hopes for recovery indeed seemed remote. Jake was not able to see. Would he be blind the rest of his life? He was not able to walk. Would he be paralyzed the rest of his life? Jake couldn't hear. Would he be deaf the rest of his life? He could not speak. Would he be a blind, deaf, mute quadriplegic? None of those questions mattered to Linda or Richard. They were just glad to see Jake alive and starting to wiggle.

Days of post-coma recovery seemed endless. All five of Jake's senses were just as numb as his four limbs. Years of rehabilitation could not be comprehended, but Linda and Richard understood the need for daily perseverance to help Jake on the journey from death's door to divinely assisted recovery. Mom Linda became Jake's daily mentor, encourager and prayer warrior. In addition, Jake's Grandma, Gladys Shadoan, was extremely diligent in prayer. She claimed healing to everyone she met. Every professional diagnosis assessed that Jake would be a vegetable, couldn't ever do this or that. Such analyses were rejected in the healing name of Christ. Grandma Shadoan and the Parker family walked by faith and not by what they saw during the slow recovery process. Linda literally stood beside Jake as he regained use of his senses: touch, smell, taste, sight and hearing. It took almost one year for Jake to see again and a couple of years to regain full speech capability. Limited mobility actually returned a full year before Jake was able to speak his first post-accident words.

Eventually, all of Jake's senses returned with heightened capacity *except* for common sense. After five years at various rehabilitation centers, Jake returned to life as normal. Normal for Jake included drugs and alcohol, addictions that had bound him since his early teen years. Incredibly, even though God had miraculously spared him from death and literally given him a third lease on life, the addictive vices once again gained control of Jake's life. ***An addict's decisions are based on deluded senses, not on what is right or on common sense.*** He got in trouble with the law, was convicted of a felony and had his driving privileges revoked. Jake stubbornly resisted God's love and yielded to the passions of the flesh.

Jake's wake-up call came when the person he loved more than any other human was beckoned to glory. Linda Parker, age 55, went to be with Jesus on November 7, 2003. She suffered a blood clot in her lungs following complications from gastric bypass

**An addict's decisions are based on deluded senses, not on what is right or on common sense.**

surgery and painlessly slipped away to an unexpected death. That great physical loss drove Jake to his knees, and he desired to repent and make changes in his life while seeking God's forgiveness. Of course, God welcomed his prodigal child, Jake, back with open arms. Years of Linda's earnest prayers were rewarded even as she enjoyed eternal rest and glory. What an amazing God who answered the faithful prayers of a loving mother after her passing from this world! Her son returned to his first love.

Jake cried every day for a couple of months and began to intensely study the Bible and pray regularly. By summer of 2004, he was sensing a burden in his heart to get involved in some type of mission work. Jake met with his pastor, Buddy Crabtree, at Union Baptist Church. Buddy gave Jake some information about various mission works and encouraged Jake to remain in prayer about this newfound desire that had been planted within him from above.

Several weeks after Jake's meeting with Pastor Buddy, I was scheduled to preach at Union Baptist Church. During that Sunday morning service, August 22, 2004, the worshippers were challenged to "live a mission life", using Paul's life account from Acts 20:19-28 as a model. In addition, we viewed a short video clip highlighting the recently completed summer mission journey to Ukraine. Jake was stirred in spirit by the sermon and presentation. We shook hands in the lobby, but I did not specifically remember meeting Jacob Parker that day.

Later that afternoon, Jake called our home, and Tanya answered. I was out of town at a speaking engagement that evening, and Tanya took a message for me to return the call. She said that a nice, older gentleman from Union Baptist Church was interested in helping us. Neither of us had remembered meeting him that morning. That next afternoon, I called Jake. From his quiet voice, I, like Tanya, pictured a soft-spoken older man, perhaps in his 50's or 60's, with limited physical abilities. I remember envisioning a weak man, perhaps confined to a wheelchair. Regardless of his stature, praise the Lord, he wanted to help MASTER Provisions on a regular basis. He could at least sit and help sort clothing to prepare it for shipments. We talked about the ministry and purpose of MP and discussed our needs for regularly sorting and packing clothing and loading containers. We agreed that Tuesday, September 7, would be a suitable first day for Jake to begin volunteer service for MP. Maybe he could assist us a day or two each week?

It was an unseasonably hot post-Labor Day Tuesday with temperatures hovering near 90 degrees. Mark Scherer and I were working together that day as we drove up to Jake's house and prepared to meet him personally for the first time. I recalled the lengthy phone conversations with a soft-spoken man. Have you ever pictured what someone would look like based on what they sounded like on the phone? I expected to see a relatively weak little man, perhaps walking with the assistance of a cane, surely stooped over and fragile and certainly eligible for senior citizen discounts.

Before I even had time to get to Jake's front door, out strode a giant of a man to meet us, dressed in a long black turtleneck sweater and long black pants. Was this a giant version of Johnny Cash clad in black attire? What a huge surprise that we were looking at a young man with obvious physical strength! It did seem like unusual attire for such a hot late summer day, but perhaps he liked to sweat. Jake hopped in the box truck, and so began our first day of work.

We discussed Jake's past. I was totally mesmerized by all of the details from drug and alcohol addictions, to the incredible pickup truck wreck, years of rehabilitation, death of his mother, meeting with Pastor Buddy, the missions call on his life, etc. What struck me the most really amounted to an indictment of Christians. Jake explained why he was dressed the way that he was on such a hot day. He has massive tattoos on his arms and back and some smaller versions on his legs. One tattoo is a large dragon, and we now joke about the little pet lizard that follows him around. Jake had prayed for several days before meeting the gang at MP that we would accept him the way he was. You see, Jake had experienced times where Christians would turn an uncaring shoulder toward him or want nothing to do with him because of those literal marks from a checkered past. How true the oft-incriminating words of 1 Samuel 16:7: "The Lord does not look at the things man looks at. Man looks at the outward appearance, but the Lord looks at the heart." Jake's tattoos remind me to always look past the visible when we encounter others. On the second day of Jake's volunteer service, we "buffeted" our bodies at lunchtime at a Chinese restaurant. After returning from the restroom, I was looking around for Jake. Back in the corner of the restaurant, I found him holding hands and praying with two of the workers. He was teaching them how to pray. Such is Jake's pattern of never being ashamed of Jesus and always being prepared to witness for Him. How refreshing to see someone so in love with Jesus that he is always ready to "raise and praise"!

Jake referred to me as Big Daddy from the very first day we met. I began to call him Big Daddy in return, but Jake noted that he was not a father. Therefore, he could not accurately be named Big Daddy. One day as we were listening to Christian music on the FM dial, a song by Big Daddy Weave hit the air. Jake loved the song, and I gave him the nickname Weave since we are as close as brothers. I'm Big Daddy. Jake is Weave. That nickname stuck, and Jake even owns some T-shirts with Weave emblazoned on the back.

Weave loved the physical work associated with MP from the very beginning. At 260 pounds and 6½ feet tall, he certainly did a lot more than just sort and fold clothes. He loved to throw around the 85-pound bags like Mom would hoist a feather pillow. After a couple of weeks, I told Jake that we needed to have a talk. The words "needed to have a talk" usually indicate problems for the "talkee"; so Weave thought he was in trouble. He surely thought he had done something wrong. Trouble nothing! The talk was scheduled to thank Jake for two great weeks of service and ask him to join MP as a full-time volunteer assistant effective October 1, 2004. As Jake would say, it was a glorious day and certainly a glorious moment. In fact, you can count on hearing the words "It's a glorious day!" from Jake as he greets you. From the time of "the talk" forward, Jake's famous "high altitude" bear hugs officially became a part of MP's repertoire of services. Weave accepted the offer to join us, and MASTER Provisions became enriched daily by the untiring efforts of a twice-dead volunteer!

# CHAPTER 10

# Friends Like Weave

Throughout MP's history, God has raised up many other people to join us in ministry. As work needs evolved, we offered staff jobs to those who were already offering their volunteer service in some manner. We did not actively recruit uninvolved outsiders to fill required positions. God put us together with many friends like Weave who already had a passion for MP's outreach to a needy world.

## TIMELY TOM

After nearly five years of donning all the hats of MP's mission work, ministry burnout loomed imminent for me. Handling speaking, packing, loading, mission trip coordination, documentation, bookkeeping, E-mails, correspondence, newsletters, etc. for a growing ministry while serving on staff at Community Christian Church left little time for family or sanity. Help was badly needed.

At that time in Canyonville, Oregon, the father of my sister-in-law was winding down a career in the Christian preaching ministry. Tom Pendergrass served churches for 44 years, mostly as a Senior Minister, in his native New Mexico, California and Oregon. By mid-summer 1998, Tom knew that his work had been fulfilled in Canyonville, and it was time to retire from the located church ministry. He informed the church eldership that he would step down at the beginning of the following year.

Tom and his wife, Barbara, had no plans to sit around and eat bon-bons until Jesus called them home. They wanted to serve together in God's Kingdom in some part-time capacity during their golden years. Tom and Barbara were faithful prayer warriors for MP since its inception and offered financial gifts as needs arose during our formative years. Their location on the West Coast limited our interaction, but we loved and respected them immensely in the Lord.

Tom and Barbara visited their Kentucky kin, daughter Paula, in November 1998. At that time, I was busy helping Paula's husband (my brother, Dave) remodel their former home that they were sprucing up to sell. Tom lent a hand for a couple of days in the construction process. I left for a mission trip to Ukraine while Tom and Barbara finished their time in Northern Kentucky. During the last few days of that visit, Tanya and Barbara chatted about the future Pendergrass plans. Barbara mentioned that they would love to get involved with a ministry like MASTER Provisions. That conversation stuck in Tanya's mind, because wives are good at knowing when their hubbies are overloaded.

Upon returning from the memorable November trip to Ukraine, Tanya mentioned her conversation with Barbara. She was right, as wives usually are. We desperately needed help at MP! At our December Board of Directors' meeting, I proposed the need for an assistant at MP to help share the administrative load. A job description was presented and approved. The search began and ended swiftly with a single, cross-country conversation with Tom Pendergrass.

The Pendergrasses had returned to Canyonville to finish their last month of service there. Tom answered that mid-December phone call. I invited him to consider a move to Kentucky to join MP as a part-time Administrative Director. The job description perfectly matched the type of work that interested Tom. Within a few days, Tom accepted the offer to join MP on April 1. We trusted that this would give them time to sell their Canyonville home, locate a new residence in Kentucky and enjoy some vacation and travel time.

Sure enough, God blessed their real estate endeavors with remarkable speed and success. The winter market in Canyonville, renowned for sales difficulty, turned up a buyer at a fair price within one month. The home in Florence, Kentucky, that Tom helped to fix and had visited occasionally became his first dwelling place east of the Mississippi River. Yes, Tom and Barbara bought Dave and Paula's home. The Pendergrasses were able to enjoy a two-month vacation, the long move was completed and Tom settled in as the second staff worker for MP.

The "part-time" portion failed to materialize quickly. Tom and Barbara jumped in with both feet from the very beginning. Tom actually served on our June 1999 mission team that took to the streets of Kakhovka, Ukraine. He got a first-hand look at the needs overseas and the impact of MP's clothing ministries. Upon his return from the mission field, Tom learned all of the aspects of support services needed to run the ministry. Within the first year, he took over all correspondence, accounting and documentation duties and surely became worthy of a title such as Timely Tom, joining MP at just the right time. He actually worked full-time on less than a part-time salary for seven years before finally moving to official part-time status in 2006. Tom and Barbara are two of the finest Christian servants that I have ever met. They have made an indelible mark on the lives of many and on the ministry of MASTER Provisions.

## JUMPIN' JIMMY

God converged the Babik and Smelser paths at First Church of Christ in Florence in January 1981. We met Jim and Tammie at the Merry Mates Bible School class led by Joe Parker. Jim jokes about "cramming" a four-year degree into five years at Cincinnati Bible College and Seminary. He decided not to enter into full-time vocational Christian service following graduation. For the first ten post-college years, Jim held two jobs in the real estate management field and a sales job. Then, he switched into personal financial management. His new business was established in Bloomington, Indiana, so the Smelsers made their nest on Route 50 in Bedford.

Jim's widowed mother welcomed them to share her property, so they moved into a mobile home on the farm. Eventually, they planned to build a non-portable structure. In the early '90's, we initiated an annual Woodcutters' Weekend, during which we would travel to the Smelser farm to cut the winter's supply of firewood. Jim called me in September 1994 to set up Woodcutters' Weekend. I told Jim it would be really difficult to join in on the logging activity that year because of MASTER Provisions, not realizing that Jim knew nothing of our fledgling mission organization. So, we chatted at length about MP, and Jim immediately solved the woodcutting dilemma. He proposed that we prepare the winter's stock of heating fodder as usual and then kick off clothing drive at his home church that Sunday. Sure enough, MP was introduced at Mt. Pleasant Christian Church as the grand finale to Woodcutters' Weekend. Jim swiftly caught on to the sorting and packing methods and managed to get the donated items ready to ship several weeks after Kickoff Sunday.

Jim got hooked on MP and excited about our mission and started spreading the word throughout Central Indiana. By the end of the first half of 1995, Jim was a regular on the MP speaking circuit. He became a devoted volunteer worker on a weekly basis. His part-time involvement continued to expand during the 90's, but Jim had no plans to leave his financial consulting business. He loved the ministry and scope of MP; it became his personal ministry and avocation.

Jim specialized in vehicle maintenance during the early years of MP's growth. He solicited help from some of Indiana's finest shade-tree mechanics and saved a lot of money for MP. We would shuttle two vehicles between Northern Kentucky and Bedford, Indiana, and transfer loads of clothing to Kentucky and take care of mechanical needs on the Indiana side. Our first school bus, a brightly colored red and white vintage beauty, showed us why school buses are normally a lemon color when it blew a radiator hose after two hours of trouble-free service. Jim picked up the nickname "Broken Bus" during those early days of MP when maintenance-free months were the exception rather than the rule. His enthusiasm for our mission as a volunteer was truly remarkable. Jim sometimes thought about how great it would be to do MP work full time, but it did not seem that we required his services on a full-time basis.

In September 1999, one of the members at Jim's home church approached Mr. Smelser and told him that he seemed like a frustrated missionary. Furthermore, he asked Jim to consider abandoning his financial services business to serve as a Development Director for a well-established mission organization. That offer triggered a careful thought and analysis process, because the proposed job would require relocation. In Jim's mind, three things would have to happen in order for him to sell his practice and move. First, a prospective buyer would have to be a devoted Christian businessman, so that he could transition his clients to a trusted worker. Second, he needed the potential buyer to guarantee employment for his valued secretary. Lastly, someone would have to take care of his mother's farm, since Jim's father was deceased.

God is really good at taking care of details! Jim moved forward in faith, believing that he was supposed to take this position of Development Director. A wonderful Christian businessman, who six months earlier had not been ready to take over Jim's financial consulting business, agreed to buy the business and hire his trusted secretary. That one offer satisfied two transition requirements. In addition, Jim's sister and brother-in-law were thrilled with the opportunity to move to the Smelser farm in Bedford. Jim then sold the business and placed an offer on a home near the mission headquarters.

That next week, Jim met with the mission's Board of Directors. Presumably, it would be a rubber stamp affair, where all questions were answered and Jim would be dubbed DD, Director of Development. However, one man at the meeting was unexpectedly demanding, lacking in grace and even a bit rude toward Jim. He was really taken back at the unexpected response but continued with the meeting. A few days later, the friend who recommended Jim for the job called to confirm Jim's start date. However, the Lord led Jim to decline the opportunity, in large part due to the unsettling comments at the meeting with the Board.

So, an unemployed Jim, who had already sold his business in anticipation of the move into missions, found himself in a major predicament. He was still performing volunteer duties for MP, and we had a trip to Tennessee scheduled for the weekend following the fiasco. During the trip, we talked about the situation and prayed about what the Lord would have us to do. Jim had invested five years of volunteer service with MP, but we were not sure that another full-time worker was needed. God set off one of those divine light bulbs in my head as we shared our hearts. There was a mission in Indianapolis that was purchasing clothes to send to Ukraine. Perhaps, they could buy the clothing from us and that would basically fund Jim's salary with MP.

Both the MASTER Provisions' board and the director of the Indianapolis-based ministry agreed it would be a great way for Jim to join MP as our third staff worker. So, in faith, Jim was offered a position as Regional Coordinator with MP in late November and began full-time work effective December 1, 1999. Plans to provide clothing for the Indiana mission never materialized because God had something better in store. New clothing ministries in Kakhovka, Brovary, and Belogorsk, Ukraine, were established within the first year after Jim joined the ranks. So, our container shipments nearly doubled from 13 to 22 during 2000. Jim was an answer to our workload needs, and God provided the funding to allow Jim to support his family financially.

Eventually, Jim was promoted from Regional Coordinator to Director of Operations and assumed responsibility for all aspects of international shipping for MP. In addition to taking care of regular clothes-packing events and speaking engagements, Jim coordinates and manages all trucking and logistics services for MP. He also assists other charitable organizations in their efforts to send relief goods overseas. Jimmy jumped into volunteer action on short notice in 1994. He then leaped into full-time service with MP on equally short call in 1999. His tireless efforts and ability to regularly jump from project to project have served as a catalyst for much of the growth MP has experienced since 2000. Jumpin' Jimmy is using his life to share the love of Jesus in practical ways within a needy world!

### MISSING MARK

When I returned to Kentucky after my second mission trip to Ukraine, we shared the story of MP and our work abroad with the church family. An enthusiastic young man was immediately interested in joining us on future trips. He seemed young even though he was in his mid-forties at the time. Mark Scherer was motivated by the presentation and eager to get involved in the field. He became a regular on MP mission trips beginning in 1997.

Between June 1997 and June 2002, Mark served with MP on ten mission trips. He returned from the 2002 journey with a huge burden on his heart. Within two weeks after returning, Mark asked to talk. He came over to our home, and we visited for several hours. Mark shared how his wife, Pam, had confirmed that he needed to leave the relative security of his business and get involved full-time with missions work. So, Mark left behind everything he had worked for in landscaping and painting businesses and began to volunteer with MP.

He relieved my burden of daily clothes pickup work in Northern Kentucky and soon became a staff member at MP. He relied on the Lord to meet his family's salary needs and began work for a pittance. Mark offered three years of faithful service and even started a teen internship ministry in Ukraine. He willingly invested two months each summer with the express purpose of showing the love of Christ to needy teens in Ukraine through soccer programs and street evangelism.

In July 2005, we sent Mark to Murfreesboro, a tiny town in central Arkansas, for a weekend speaking and preaching assignment. Mark flew into Little Rock, rented a car and was scheduled to arrive in Murfreesboro at 6:00 p.m. to meet the preacher for supper. About 9:00 p.m., my cell phone chimed and Mike Rathbone, Senior Minister at First Christian Church, was on the horn. He asked if Mark was running late. I told him it would be unusual for Mark to be late and offered to attempt to contact him. Mark's cell phone service was not available in rural Arkansas, so my efforts proved futile. Attempts to reach Pam were equally unsuccessful, so Mike and I agreed to get in touch with each other if we obtained any information on Mark's whereabouts. Mike waited patiently for over five hours at a restaurant adjacent to the hotel where Mark was to stay. He had already gone into the front desk and asked if Mark had checked in. He was informed that they had not seen him.

Detective Babik initiated some investigative work. The Delta flight had arrived without incident, and Mark was aboard, so I called the rental car counter at the Little Rock airport to see if Mr. Scherer had visited them. Sure enough, he had rented the car between 3 and 4:00 p.m. Since it's less than a two-hour drive from Little Rock to "the Murf", we wondered if Mark might have experienced car trouble or worse. Pastor Mike initiated a request for State Police to check on any accidents on the route between the airport and his destination. By 11:30 p.m., Mike checked one more time at the hotel to see if they had heard from Mark and received a negative response. He left a note with the attendant and turned in for the night after we chatted.

About that time, I finally reached Pam and explained the situation to her. She did not know whether to laugh or cry. Instead, she committed to pray and to get others praying for Mark. We had actually called the credit card center and found that Mark had charged a meal at 9:00 p.m. about 15 miles south of his intended destination. Maybe he was just lost, we thought, but why was he still not back to the hotel at 11:30 when he finished the seafood supper at 9:00 p.m.? Mike received the information and had the state police thoroughly comb the 15 miles of road between the restaurant and hotel. There were still no signs of Mark. We all tried to sleep that night, but it was certainly a restless night for many. Pam spent the entire night in prayer without any shuteye.

The next morning, Mike went to the hotel and found Mark enjoying breakfast and some caffeine in the lobby. Mike immediately called me, I notified Pam and then Mark and his bride caught up on the past 24 hours. The series of events that had occurred was amazing.

A huge storm had hit the area after Mark checked into the hotel. He had been registered electronically in the system. However, the power outage plus a shift change occurred between Mark's check-in time and the times that Mike had asked about Mark's arrival. The new attendant was not aware that Mr. Scherer was in town. They could not access the computer records. Mark had tried to call the Rathbones, but their phone was not working, and he had no alternate way to get in touch with them. Mark and Mike had waited for each other for supper within 150 feet of each other, and Mark finally went to a recommended restaurant in an adjacent town. He returned to the hotel by 10:00 p.m. and fell sound asleep while everyone who loved him wondered of his whereabouts and prayed. Mark reported that it was an exceptional night of sleep, perhaps the best he ever recalled. *Apparently, all of the prayers for his safety and protection served as heavenly sleeping pills.*

That July night, when we envisioned Mark involved in a potentially fatal car wreck on the side of an Arkansas mountain, served as a foreshadow of what transpired on December 5, 2005. Late that evening, Mark's life changed in the instant that Pam swerved to miss a deer on the winding road near their home. The ensuing head-on collision with a tree nearly claimed her life. Air Care lifted her traumatized body to University Hospital in Cincinnati and survival efforts commenced minutes after her arrival in the Neuro Intensive Care unit. Hospital medical personnel prepared the family for the worst, as we stood around our unconscious friend's motionless body to hear the rough news. They said that Pam would be paralyzed for the rest of her life, and she might not make it through the night.

We prayed urgently for God's help and, in faith, claimed God's healing touch on Pam. Minutes turned into hours, days

**Apparently, all of the prayers for his safety and protection served as heavenly sleeping pills.**

and weeks and Pam's recovery confounded the medical experts. She was able to return home in less than three months, and we believe that some day she will walk again by God's power and healing mercy.

Mark provided amazing daily care and comfort for Pam and showed us what true love and devotion to one's spouse is all about. Prior to the accident, Mark had decided to pursue studies in Radiation Technology and leave MP. Pam and Mark both want to continue those plans when the time is right. Mr. Scherer filled a vital role for MASTER Provisions, and we will always be missing Mark as we recount all of the pleasant memories of his three and one half years of service.

## DOCTOR DAVE

In the sand lands of Central Florida and the hills of Kentucky, David Bailey Mayer was reared in a God-fearing Christian home. Dave achieved mechanical geek status early in life and amazed adults with his technical abilities. In fact, he was so intrigued by mechanical devices from his earliest years that his first word was not Mama or Dada, but rather, fan. By age seven, Dave was tinkering with anything motorized. He envisioned himself involved in some type of ministry that involved speaking and mechanical work. Dave became an excellent self-taught mechanic. In addition to those valuable skills, Dave learned to mimic engine sounds. He can actually entertain audiences as people ask for a year and make of the car, and Dave imitates the noise that emanates from that vehicle's motor.

As a potential third generation physician, Dave was raised with every opportunity to pursue a career in the medical field. He never felt direct pressure to become Doctor Dave #3, but that self-imposed expectation hovered over him during his formative years. He developed musical skills and was a regular at church and youth services. Upon graduating from Wayne County High School in South Central Kentucky, Dave landed at his parents' alma mater, Milligan College, in East Tennessee. His folks, David and Helen (Bunton) Mayer attended Milligan during the same decade that Tanya and I roamed the Buffalo Mountain region.

Dave pursued a Biology major during college, although he was not convinced that the medical profession was for him. He was equally eager to study opportunities with the opposite gender and was especially attracted to a young lass named Julie Roth. Dave and Julie quickly fell in love and did the things that potential spouses do like talking about life goals, vocations, family plans, etc. Julie loved the idea of missions and teaching children, and Dave could still envision working with his hands in some type of ministry or missions work.

We first met in March 2001, when Milligan hosted a MASTER Provisions' container event. Julie became quickly enthused about the project and was more faithful than any other student in helping to sort and pack clothing for needy people abroad. She dragged Dave along during the third workday, and he soon caught the MP vision, too. Dave became an advocate for our cause and he would grab some Milligan students and "volunteer" them to help on an impromptu basis as work needs arose. Julie and Dave "double-handedly" allowed us to successfully complete that project. We parted after thanks and a pizza party, not knowing whether our paths would ever cross again.

One year later, Milligan invited me to speak at one of the college's bi-weekly convocation services. I challenged the students to follow God's call in their lives and to specifically consider full-time vocational Christian service. That week, Dave and Julie led the student initiative to help us sort, pack and load enough clothing and footwear to fill an entire container. Their servant hearts were so evident as we battled inclement weather and completed the project in spite of obstacles.

At the end of the workweek, Dave and I met for a specific purpose. We sat in the Student Union Building and chatted about Dave serving with MASTER Provisions upon graduation from Milligan. He received a not-so-lucrative job offer, consistent with MP's package for all prospective staff workers: no guaranteed pay, no benefit or retirement package, just lots of satisfaction and trusting God to provide a living wage through loving individuals and churches.

Dave was elated by the offer and agreed to prayerfully consider mission work with MP. A medical career held no special allure for Dave, and work as a missionary satisfied his inner heart's desire. At MP, Dave could use his incredible, God-given, mechanical skills that were finely honed at Milligan, where he served as unpaid campus fix-it man. With MASTER Provisions, Dave could also drive the big rigs to transport shipping containers; travel and speak at churches; and enjoy mission service abroad. The very things that Dave dreamed about as a young boy, speaking and offering mechanical skills, could be fulfilled as part of the MP team.

Dave kicked around a couple of sales and delivery jobs after graduating from Milligan in May 2002. He and Julie married in July of that same year in a lovely ceremony capped off by an exit in a horse-drawn carriage. After the honeymoon, Dave started making contacts with people to let them know that he would begin serving with MP in January 2003. The most difficult phase of mission work began: the support-raising period. Dave started working on part-time pay with full-time duties while Julie finished school during the first half of 2003. We realized that Dave would be much more useful and effective for MP if he could relocate from East Tennessee to Northern Kentucky, and he immediately agreed to move.

God provided free lodging for the newlyweds in Kentucky. The Mayers moved into a humble single-bedroom cottage out in the "boone docks". Dave's value to MP quickly manifested itself through faithful service under the hoods and engines of disabled trucks, vans and cars and thousands of miles logged behind an 18-wheeler's steering column. And, of course, Dave traveled to conduct clothes work and other mission service. Doctor Dave enjoys serving the Great Physician through ministry at MP!

## DEDICATED DON

Don Davisson served in located ministries for 40 years in Tennessee, Kentucky, Indiana and Ohio. During the 90's, we became acquainted with Don and Carolyn through their son, Terre, and daughter-in-law, Mary. Whenever the elder Davissons came to visit the kids and grandchildren in Northern Kentucky, they brought along a load of shoes and clothing collected at their home church in Nelsonville, Ohio. By 1997, Don offered to conduct a community clothes campaign in conjunction with the area Ministerial Alliance. I headed to Nelsonville and the area churches helped us pack enough goods to fill one third of a container.

While working at Nelsonville's second community clothing event, I invited Don to travel with us on a mission trip to Ukraine in November 2000. Don eagerly agreed to join the mission team to teach and preach in Ukraine in addition to ordaining nine church members into the pastorate. During the journey, Don was able to meet a lot of the Ukrainian clothing directors and came away totally enthused about the impact of MASTER Provisions' overseas ministries.

After returning home to Nelsonville, Don expanded his volunteer activities tremendously. They began weekly pickups of used clothing and footwear from a consignment shop in Athens and recruited regular volunteers to help process the donated items. Don mobilized members from four Nelsonville churches to offer their assistance. He worked to obtain donated workspace at a local historical building that was sitting vacant. Over the next two years, we were able to load four containers of goods in Nelsonville thanks to Don's volunteer efforts.

Don was perhaps our most devoted volunteer ever. In early 2002, as MP continued rapid growth, we met to discuss the possibility of Don joining us full time after retiring from the local church ministry. From the time of our initial discussion, Don eagerly anticipated the day when he could join our ranks. He began fundraising efforts that summer and announced his retirement from church ministry effective in January 2003. God blessed that decision. Don and Carolyn received free rent during their first year in Northern Kentucky with MP! Don is renowned as a master shoe packer. The quality of packing boxes of footwear sent overseas is measured against Don's standards and "Donny Box" means a superbly packed shoebox. Don takes care of our newsletter mailings and other administrative support services. Don and Carolyn are investing their golden years in dedicated service to the Lord!

CHAPTER *11*

# *Glorious Growth*

Expansion of mission ministry is accomplished in partnership with other people, churches and ministries. ***We are committed to "territorial enlargement" only when God supplies the connections to us.*** In other words, MP grows as God brings people and situations to our attention. We do not actively seek new outreach opportunities. By waiting on the Lord, we know that He is linking us with situations and people instead of wondering if it is mere human effort on our part as opposed to divine assistance. We are very comfortable waiting on God, and He has provided glorious growth to MASTER Provisions over the years.

Throughout the first six years of ministry, our output was limited to shipments of used clothing and footwear to Ukraine.

**We are committed to "territorial enlargement" only when God supplies the connections to us.**

After Jim and Tom joined the staff and we were positioned to handle additional work, a tide of new opportunity rolled in during Y2K. Jim obtained a Commercial Driver's License to allow him to drive semi-tractors. Accordingly, MP began to save big bucks by not having to pay professional trucking companies to transport our shipping containers. As seasoned administrators of international logistics and shipping operations, we began to offer our services at greatly reduced rates to other mission organizations. MASTER Provisions could then serve as a total logistics coordinator and supplier to help other ministries save money while sending relief goods overseas. As alliances were forged with missionaries in new fields, we simply offered to ship containers of clothing and footwear and relied on foreign leaders to make all decisions relating to distribution procedures, donation guidelines, job creation, ministry outreach methods, etc.

Kosova as well as Bosnia and Herzegovina, two of the six countries that evolved from Yugoslavia's breakup, were our first two countries added to the shipping schedule after the turn of the millennium. (Bosnia and Herzegovina is the official name of one country even though it sounds like two countries.) Kosova was the first country outside of Ukraine to receive MP shipments in 2001. Our partners there work in a predominately Islamic country to help restore life in that war-torn region. They show the love of Jesus to people through various humanitarian assistance programs like clothing, cow provision, home building and well construction. LifeSpring Christian Church (formerly Clovernook Christian Church) in Cincinnati partners with us to send occasional shipments to Bosnia and Herzegovina.

In 2002, we met a Belarussian pastor who serves a Russian-speaking church in Cincinnati, Ohio. Konstantin was excited about joining us in a project to help people in Belarus, one of the 15 countries established after the fall of the Soviet Union. Konstantin worked out details with customs authorities in Belarus and mobilized a group of Methodist churches in the Wapakoneta, Ohio, region to collect, pack and load the first clothing container for shipment to Belarus.

Belarussian officials quoted customs fees of $2,500 in order to clear the container, and that is actually a very reasonable assessment in comparison to charges leveled by other countries. The Wapak project went well, and the shipment headed overseas. However, the troubles began when the container arrived in Minsk, the capital city. Greedy customs representatives decided that clearance fees needed to be increased fivefold. Consequently, the container contents were destined to sit in storage in Minsk until more money could be tendered. Over the next few months, some lenders in Belarus came to the rescue and offered the additional $10,000.

When our friends approached the customs officials with the new clearance fees, the requirements had changed again. Our documents stated that all clothing originated from the USA, meaning it was collected and packed in the States, not manufactured here. The crooked customs people said that our partners in Belarus would have to prove that the clothing was made in the U.S., not just packed there, in order to release the container from customs' control. Their proposed test was simple. Three large bags of clothing would be opened, and every piece of clothing with a tag must say that the clothing was "Made in the USA". An average of 150 garments per bag is typical. Now, if you have ever looked through your wardrobe and glanced at the manufacturer's tags, you realize that the majority of clothing in your closet is made in many different countries. God chose to do a miracle to show His power. As the customs officials examined nearly 500 pieces of clothing, they could find none with tags for threads made anywhere other than the USA. Miraculous indeed! The container was released to our friends and thousands of needy people in Belarus received good, used clothing and shoes.

Dave Mayer joined the ranks in 2003 and provided an additional semi-truck driver to help with increased transportation needs as MP experienced tremendous expansion of operations. We entered into a partnership with the National Missionary Convention that year, where teens from the convention help to process and prepare enough clothing to fill a shipping container. Conference attendees bring donated items to help the cause. During the first four years of partnership with the NMC, containers were shipped to Ukraine, Sudan, India and Romania.

In early 2004, Jesus Shine Ministries in central India learned about MP on the Internet and asked us to consider helping them. We checked several references, and I talked to a man who had personally visited their work several times. JSM assists widows and orphans to meet food and clothing needs while they teach the Gospel in and around the huge city of Hyderabad, India. We planned to load three containers in Lansing, Michigan, on September 11, 2004, as part of MP's largest annual clothing extravaganza. One of those three shipments was earmarked for JSM.

A small team joined me on an MP-sponsored trip to India from December 2–14. After spending 18 hours on two long flights and 17 hours in a painfully cramped van, we arrived at an evangelistic meeting on a Saturday night in Hyderabad. Nearly 1,800 Indians waited for several hours past our targeted arrival time and listened intently as I shared the Gospel message. Afterwards, they lined up to receive a bag of clothing from the shipment packed in Lansing several months earlier. This scene repeated itself twelve other times during the next ten days in India. When we were ready to depart, one half of a container of used clothing and shoes remained. The leaders of JSM asked us if we had any preference about how to distribute the goods. We said we were certain that God would show them what to do.

Sure enough, December 26, 2004, became a date firmly ensconced in natural disaster history. A gigantic tsunami struck Southeast Asia and claimed hundreds of thousands of lives. Survivors along the shores of southeast India lost every earthly possession. Jesus Shine Ministries became one of the first relief organizations on site to pass out tons of clothing and footwear to desperately needy people. None of us working in four parking lots of L&L Food Stores in Lansing, Michigan, on September 11, a date rife with its own tragedy, knew the good work that God had planned for all of the clothing and shoes. God led JSM to contact us, and He led MP to send one of the Michigan containers to India. Accordingly, JSM was prepared in advance to do the good work of assisting thousands of suffering fellow citizens, who received needed shoes and clothing in Jesus' name. We never know what God will do with our acts of service and kindness, do we? We praise Him for preparing people in Michigan to take care of tsunami survivors in India.

In October of 2004, faculty members at Gray Middle School in Union, Kentucky, approached us about the possibility of helping to send a shipment of clothing, shoes and paperback books to Iraq. Used books would be given to U.S. troops. Service men and women would distribute clothing to needy Iraqis. Such charity helps to build relational bridges in the Baghdad region. Chris Bassett, a devoted Army chaplain, arranged for the shipment and secured friends and churches in the U.S. to pay for the shipment. Students at Gray Middle School and Ryle High School teamed up with area residents to donate clothing and books. Gray students helped us to sort, pack and load part of the container on a school day just before the Christmas break. The project was extremely successful, and we finished loading our first shipment to Iraq on a bitterly cold Saturday morning in January 2005.

U.S. military transportation specialists eventually trucked the container from Kuwait to Camp Victory, Iraq, as conditions allowed. All of the goods were distributed in the summer of 2005, and the shipping container that was purchased, as opposed to rented, now meets storage needs in Iraq. Officer Bassett's emails and encouraging words about God's amazing protection and provision over our troops that he had witnessed while serving in Iraq were very moving and inspiring. We thank God for committed Christians willing to put their lives on the line and their faith into practice in the most difficult of circumstances!

God's perfect provision has been displayed countless times over the years. Some of His amazing works on our behalf relate to control of the weather. During one of the huge, outdoor events in Lansing, Michigan, weather forecasters called for 100% chance of rain. The publicized work times were 8:00 a.m. until 4:00 p.m. Dark clouds surrounded the area during the entire day, and people drove up with cars still wet from driving through rain showers. Many folks expressed surprise that we were still working outdoors. However, not one drop fell in the parking lot turned clothes command central. We finished loading the container just prior to 4:00 p.m. and completed clean up exactly two minutes before the skies overhead unleashed a torrential downpour. God kept us dry when everyone else in the area was wet!

God provided an encore performance in Plainfield, Indiana. We set up an outdoor work area even though the forecast called for heavy rains. Occasional rays of sunshine splashed onto the Plainfield Christian Church parking lot off and on during that day and dark clouds seemed to break up and move around the area. People driving up to donate clothing were amazed to see us working outside as they arrived with cars that had been driven through nature's car wash. Within five minutes after closing the doors on the loaded container, the thunder rolled and rains pelted the complex. God chose to keep His clothing and workers dry until the job was completed!

SouthEast Christian Church in Louisville, Kentucky, started working with us in 2001 to ship containers to their mission affiliate in Simferopol, Ukraine. The first annual event featured hundreds of members dropping off donated items during an October Sunday. At the announced quitting time, we were several bags short and ready to close the container. Some people drove up in a van with just enough shoes and clothing to perfectly fill the remaining space at the back of the shipping unit.

God has a good track record for nick-of-time provisioning. During the first Plainfield Christian Church initiative to fill an entire container in the 90's, we hustled to get all of the goods processed and loaded before the volunteers departed. We ended up with just enough space in which to squeeze two, five-year old kids when all of the dust settled. Just as we were shutting the door, an elderly couple drove up with four large brightly colored yellow bags. The bags appeared designed for the empty space. We captured the moment on film. A ministry video shows the container door closing, bright yellow bags jammed in on the top row, and a group of tired workers cheering wildly.

Many times during the past 12 years, we have arrived to pick up clothing with vehicles or trailers that represented our best guess as to what storage capacity would be needed. There always seems to be just enough space to handle the load. Back in the mid to late 90's, we finished our first annual clothing project in Ft. Wayne, Indiana. We selected a 24-foot truck to haul ocean-ready goods back to the Northern Kentucky warehouse. After several days of work, we finished loading the truck, but thirty boxes would not fit. Rather than leaving some items behind, we took a page right from Jethro's moving manual, in which safety takes a back seat to necessity. We pulled the steel-loading ramp out seven feet beyond the back of the truck and wedged wood pieces into either side between the ramp and frame. Then, we tied rope from the ramp handles onto the truck's frame. Thirty boxes were strapped onto the makeshift platform, and we completed the 200-mile jaunt back to Kentucky without incident or police intervention.

MP launched the MASTER Care orphan placement ministry in 2003 as a means to offer adoptive Christian homes to precious children living in Ukrainian orphanages. The concept for this exciting outreach ministry was birthed in the compassionate and innovative hearts of Dr. Greg Koo and Joe Parker. They evaluated the feasibility of this type of ministry during their 2003 trip to Ukraine. The Bible tells us that caring for widows and orphans is the ultimate expression of pure and undefiled religion (James 1:27). Therefore, the ministry would be based on orphan care. Families in Ukraine, approved by a board of 25 pastors, permanently adopt young orphaned children and U.S. sponsors donate money that is given to the Ukrainian family. At its inception,

MASTER Care families received a monthly support gift of fifty dollars. That money helps with expenses and takes some pressure off mothers, who feel compelled to find outside work in order to make ends meet.

Our ministry partner for orphan care in Ukraine is called My Home. The My Home directors conduct regular home visits as they distribute monthly support stipends. MP passes along all monies donated by sponsors, and the adoptive families are blessed with much-needed income to help them provide necessities for their families. About one child per month is placed into a Christian home in Ukraine.

Our first MASTER Care placement involved a young boy named Ivan, or John, from an orphanage in the Kherson region. The adopting father is a pastor named Anatoly, who serves in the village of Gornostayevka. Several years before they adopted John, Anatoly and his wife, Galla, experienced the ultimate pain in life. Their four-year old biological son, Ivan, died due to accidentally ingesting some highly poisonous mushrooms. Certainly, their new John will never replace their beloved Ivan, but he fills a little hole in their hearts. The Ponomarevs are gracious and joyful people and offer a marvelous home environment for their precious MASTER Care child.

MP is open to expanding MASTER Care into other countries if God brings people to us who are able to establish the adoption procedures in their home nations. It took about six months to overcome governmental obstacles in Ukraine and complete the first placement. New programs are notoriously slow in getting started in most countries. We would also expect MASTER Care programs in other nations to develop slowly, but the opportunities to take the operating concept to other nations are seemingly endless.

Throughout the years of glorious growth, our primary focus has centered on assisting needy people in economically devastated countries through clothing and other benevolent ministries. However, we were compelled to bend our primary mission a bit to get involved with some stateside assistance in 2005. Our nation experienced a devastating natural calamity when Hurricane Katrina came calling in August of that year. Millions of volunteer hours were needed to help the survivors in clean up and rebuilding efforts. A MASTER Provisions volunteer, a "young-at-heart" man named Marvin Heinemann, approached us in October with a ministry idea.

Marvin wanted to share the love of Jesus with children in the bayou area by collecting a semi-trailer filled with Christmas toys and relief goods. Then, we would lead a mission team to Louisiana and Mississippi to distribute the donated items during the week before Christmas. Two local schools, Gray Middle School and Ryle High School, in Union, Kentucky, agreed to help in the collection efforts. In addition, a local business allowed us to use their parking lot as a donation drop-off point. A team of 23 students and adults agreed to journey southward the week before Christmas to spread the love of Jesus as we celebrated His birth.

The visit to the battered coast was certainly memorable. One day was perhaps more memorable than the rest. Three days before Christmas, we passed out tons of toys, food and bottled water at a tent village that housed nearly 1,000 homeless Mississippians. One non-English speaking lady was overcome with emotion as we erected a Christmas tree outside of her tent and gave her a sack of gifts for her family. Her buoyant smile transcended the language barrier as she hugged us and said "gracias". Our Katrina

Christmas venture turned into a marvelous ministry opportunity, and we will always cherish those memories.

*Outstanding mission partnerships are regularly established through God-ordained circumstances.* Then, they blossom over time as two groups work together to accomplish God's purposes. Our wonderful relationship with the Southern Heights Christian Church, of Lebanon, Missouri, illustrates how a partnership is born and thrives.

In 2001, Jay Horn, former MP employee, and I coached a home school basketball team. Our year-end celebration and challenge included a jaunt to Oklahoma City to participate in a national tournament. Both Jay and I are fiscal conservatives, or more aptly stated, cheapskates, so we contemplated money-saving travel options. One idea involved checking with a church to see if they might impart compassion to low-income wayfarers passing through their region. We mathematically calculated the halfway point of the two-day transit to fall somewhere in central to western Missouri.

A careful map analysis revealed that Lebanon was an ideal mid-point for the journey. Two weeks prior to our departure, we consulted a national church directory and located the Southern Heights church. A phone call to their office was greeted with a spirit of willing helpfulness. The church secretary immediately referred us to Bill and Frances Adams, who served on the missions committee. Mr. and Mrs. Adams welcomed our call and displayed gracious hospitality to complete strangers. They

**Outstanding mission partnerships are regularly established through God-ordained circumstances.**

offered to house our entourage at the church building and help us to prepare supper and breakfast. In addition, we told Bill and Frances about MASTER Provisions, and they agreed to host an impromptu mission committee meeting so we could tell them about MP during our brief stay in the Show-Me State.

The trip, which included a second-place finish in the basketball tournament, had presented a divine opportunity for us to forge new relationships. The mission team at Southern Heights responded to our presentation with great interest. We agreed to keep in touch with each other. Within 15 months of our rendezvous in Lebanon, Southern Heights Christian Church began to financially support MP.

Their ministry involvement level has multiplied continually over the years. In addition to increasing monetary gifts, Southern Heights started to sponsor a MASTER Care child soon after the ministry was unveiled in 2003. By the end of 2005, the church sponsored five adopted children. Southern Heights found out about the need for milk for malnourished children in Zimbabwe. They offered enough money to provide milk for over ten thousand poor Zimbabweans. They plan to send people with us on future mission trips and several of their members also offer extremely generous financial gifts above and beyond giving to MP from the mission budget.

Bill and Frances Adams are incredible ambassadors and partners for MP. They initiated and coordinated a plan to start collecting, sorting and packing clothing year round in Lebanon in 2003. Through their leadership, the church now fills a couple of clothing containers each year. Mr. and Mrs. Adams also served as one of our initial individual sponsors in MASTER Care. The little girl that they support, Veronika, is a living miracle saved from certain death moments after being birthed into an outdoor toilet. In addition to being spared from physical death, Veronika received a new spiritual lease on life as she was placed into a wonderful Christian home in Ukraine in 2003. Bill and Frances provide the financial sponsorship to assist the Ukrainian family as they raise Veronika in the ways of the Lord. God must have a special plan for Veronika!

What powerful impact of a growing mission partnership! Southern Heights Christian Church and Bill and Frances Adams put their faith into practice. Tens of thousands of needy people have received clothing; that same number of children enjoyed a cup of milk, one special girl received a new home, and many lives will never be the same. We praise God for a loving partnership that has grown to "Southern Heights"!

# CHAPTER 12

# *Intercontinental Encounters*

---

Shipments of clothing, shoes and other relief goods offered by MASTER Provisions built a foundation for marvelous relationships and outreach overseas. During the glorious years of ministry growth, many mission experiences have helped me to grow personally because they challenged my faith and trust in God. Please enjoy some selected stories, presented in chronological order, intended to communicate the impact of clothing and humanitarian assistance in needy countries and the powerful memories created during mission encounters.

## 28-YEAR SACRIFICE

Memories of my first preaching experience at a House of Prayer in Ukraine are vivid. An old church house was filled with solemn worshipers on a Wednesday night. Those unable to find seating took advantage of standing room only locations around the inside perimeter of the small sanctuary. The fervor and seriousness of the members was impressive. The Ukrainians were in no hurry to finish the service or meet a traditional ending time. After sharing a message from my heart, two other Ukrainian pastors preached. I talked after services with many different people.

An elderly gentleman with a long gray beard patiently waited his turn to visit. He thanked me for sharing from the Gospel with their church. An amazing glow radiated from his face. He was the most angelic looking man I had ever seen, and I simply asked him about his life. He talked about the privilege that he had to suffer for the Gospel of Christ. During Communist years, it was not permissible to own a Bible or to publicly share about your faith in Jesus. But, he determined that he loved Jesus more than he feared man. So, he regularly taught others about Jesus and preached to co-workers. Three different times during his life, he was imprisoned because he continued to proclaim the Gospel after being warned to stop. The first two imprisonments lasted ten years each. His third and final period of captivity was an eight-year sentence. Our eyes filled with tears as we shared from our hearts. I was totally humbled to talk to an older brother in Christ who sacrificed 28 years of earthly freedom for the sake of our Lord.

### SHOPPING RISKS

Mission trips typically end with an opportunity for team members to buy gifts and souvenirs for loved ones and supporters. The November 1996 Ukraine team was eager for such chances, and they did such a good job of taking care of business that they found an extra two hours on their hands before needing to return to the Odessa airport. One of the team members was extremely eager to get home to family and not thrilled with the idea of an extra tourist stop intended to kill time. However, womanly rights prevailed, and we allowed an additional gift-hunting excursion.

The ladies stretched the two-hour time limit to the max, and we returned to the taxi greeted by a little and not-so pleasant surprise. One of the rear tires was totally flat. (It looked like zero percent inflation!) With no spare tire available, the driver smiled and showed us a bicycle tire pump. If you have ever tried to inflate an automobile tire with a bike pump, you understand the physical workout that faced us. Several of us lined up to take turns on the twenty-minute project. However, the one traveler most longing for home, relied on adrenaline power to complete most of the reps required in record time. The canister on the bicycle pump was blazing hot, but the tire was sufficiently filled to get us back to the airport a few minutes before we would have missed the flight cutoff. Oh, the risks associated with shopping here, there or anywhere!

## FLUSH LIGHT

MP's inaugural summer mission trip to Ukraine headed eastward in June 1997. That close-knit dynamic dozen invested time in two Southern Ukrainian towns. We invested two days in Kherson to help the large Christian Church there convert a vacated school building into a worship and educational facility. Our light construction foray included some sanding and painting teams.

The "sanders" were forced to figure out how to smooth out old wooden benches and chairs without using sandpaper. So, primitive methods were employed. Broken glass bottles served as portable sanding devices powered by elbow grease. When the sharp edge of a bottle became too smooth, a new bottle was broken to provide a more suitable sanding edge. Regular sandpaper was thought to be ineffective because it wore out too quickly. Never mind that glass bottles leave ridges in the wood. The sanders did their best but the technique was foreign to all of them, and they did more of a number on fingers than on the wood.

The painters actually thought they were doing a good job even though the paint was a little runny. Mark Scherer, formerly a professional painter, was the team Rembrandt. He was performing in spectacular fashion as fresh paint was applied to the dingy walls in several church classrooms. The Ukrainian job foreman was not impressed with Mark's efforts, though. Without the use of an interpreter, he knelt down with his head to the floor and pointed to the far underside of the hot water pipes located four inches off the floor. Not even a church mouse could ever have noticed that unpainted area. It was sad to see the foreman squabbling about what he viewed as unacceptable painting. Mark probably felt like dumping a can of paint on his head and Mark's wife, Pam, was clearly agitated on behalf of her husband. I observed the evolving situation and decided to interject a few pieces of my mind. Since there were no interpreters in sight, it seemed that some comic relief was in order. While smiling, I spoke loudly to the foreman, "You are crazy." Continuing to smile, I ranted, "Your toilets in the building don't work, and you are upset about the unpainted underside of pipes. Please fix the toilets and leave our workers alone. Do you understand?" The foreman nodded, smiled back and said, "Dah, dah, dah", meaning "Yes, yes, yes", in Russian. Obviously, we did not understand each other, so I'm sure he thought I was agreeing with him and chastising our worker. Mark, Pam and I about busted guts in laughter, and the tension was gone.

The toilet situation in the building really was untidy. There was no electricity or running water in the building, and 400 people met there for worship weekly amidst the construction mess. The indoor toilets were, quite frankly, a stinky mess. They were indoor outhouses without stools so perhaps you could call them "inhouses". Our team lodged in the facility, and many of us enjoyed rustic camping on the roof of the building. One of our female group members had to use the inhouse in the middle of the night, so she borrowed an expensive mag light from Kenny Hicks. Ken's brother-in-law lent him the light for trip use with special instructions to take good care of it. In obvious haste to complete her business on the squatty potty, she accidentally dropped the flashlight into the muck. With great embarrassment, she returned to Kenny and explained the predicament.

The potty plight was shared with a group of guys. It was hard not to laugh when Kenny said he needed some help. We engaged the assistance of a fearless friend, Greg Lyon, and took him to the disaster site. We felt our way along the walls and finally turned the corner into the bathroom and were surprised to see light. We entered the danger zone and looked into the hole and saw a beam of light shooting straight up from the mire onto the ceiling. The mag light was lodged in upright position about a foot below the surface. After sharing a hearty laugh, Kenny convinced us that he had to return home from the mission trip with the light. At a minimum, we had to try to get it.

None of us were willing to stick our hands directly into the ecological hazard. Instead, we scrounged around and found a wire coat hanger. Greg converted it into a type of "poopy" penlight retriever and began the recovery process. After about five minutes, his valiant efforts were rewarded. The mag light surfaced and Greg flipped it into the corner. But, how could we get it cleaned off? We worked our way into the building's food preparation area and grabbed a kitchen towel. I used it to gingerly pick up the nasty light source. We drew some water from a bucket in the kitchen and doused the mag light a number of times and wiped it off as best we could. We hoped that the kitchen crew would not use the towel for dishes the next day, and Kenny was relieved that the "flush" light had been saved.

The flush light episode was one that aroused much laughter over the years. Greg Lyon, hero of the dramatic rescue, always longed to resurface memories of that Ukraine mission trip as we kibitzed over the years. Greg dreamed about one day moving to a ranch in Ukraine to enjoy a simple life. Those dreams were short-circuited when my dear friend, Greg Lyon, at age 45, was taken into glory in December 2004 due to a massive heart attack. In the literal twinkling of an eye, a jewel of a man and father of four got promoted to a heavenly residence much sooner than any of us expected. Although never getting to enjoy another mission trip adventure together, we'll raise some praise at the team reunion in heaven, where flush lights will not be required.

## FOGGY MEMORIES

Mission trips such as the November 1997 jaunt to Ukraine are always motivating, memorable and enjoyable. Extremely unusual weather blanketed the entire country of Ukraine. A dense fog mass converged on Odessa, our targeted arrival site. Jim Smelser and I left Frankfurt, Germany, on schedule, not knowing the adventure that awaited us. Upon approach to Ukraine, the flight captain spoke four words in broken English that prick the hearts of even the most frequent flyers: "We have bad news." A collective gasp was heard but the news was actually very minor bad news. Air traffic controllers were diverting the landing to Kiev, an eight-hour bus ride from Odessa. Ukraine Air offered a 1960's model bus to transport all ticketed passengers from Kiev to Odessa. We were instructed to use the restrooms at the Kiev airport, because the airlines could not let us out of the bus during the long trip to Odessa for security reasons. Since the bus was devoid of necessary facilities, that request seemed a bit of a stretch.

Sure enough, four hours into the overnight bus ride from Kiev to Odessa, the driver's bladder was sufficiently stretched. We were instructed to remain seated during the stop. Right! Imagine 50 passengers on a cramped bus remaining seated while watching the driver head to the adjacent field to take care of business. Everyone stormed the exits and created one of the funniest scenes in the history of missions travel. Visibility was very poor due to the fog as the full moon tried to work its rays through the airborne water particles. That selected stretch of road had hundreds of trees. Many strategically selected trees immediately served as portable facilities. It was hilarious to see the fuzzy outlines of 50 people simultaneously standing or squatting next to a tree to "unload" on that damp, eerie night. We all re-boarded and repeated the scene one more time further along the road to Odessa with no regard for a farcical airline security policy.

Jim and I finally limped into our destination in Odessa, 14 hours after our scheduled arrival time. We had no idea how to get from Odessa to Kakhovka in the middle of the night, since our driver was supposed to meet us the day before. After exiting customs, we were stunned and amazed to find a missionary friend, Glen Elliott, patiently waiting to give us a ride to our final destination.

Our friends, Mark Scherer and Chip Vater, had planned to arrive concurrently with us on this mission trip even though they were traveling on airline standby passes. Fortunately, Jim and I had confirmed seats. Due to the weather-induced flight delays and cancellations from Germany into Ukraine, they were not able to claim any vacant seats until a flight two days later than originally planned. They invested those days trying to grab rest in airport lounges and finally arrived in Kakhovka after midnight on Friday night. Jim and I were already adjusted to life in Ukraine and had a night of sleep under our collective belts when Chip and Mark pulled into town. Needless to say, they were both extremely exhausted from two sleepless nights of travel.

Plans devised by Mr. Smelser and I were more mischievous than compassionate. All four of us were to sleep crammed together in the small living room. We had gone to bed around midnight trying to stay awake to greet our brothers. The slaphappy mind tends to be abnormally creative. Breathe-wrong nasal strips were invented that night in anticipation of our cohorts' arrival. These nasal strips are made of duct tape, a missionary's universal fix-it friend. Two very narrow strips of duct tape four inches long are attached to both sides of the mid-forehead. The strips are criss-crossed and attached to each opposite nostril, then pulled up and tightened to create a pig-like snout appearance. The practical and functional design was intended to further open nostril passages and restrict snoring.

After I installed the first-ever manufactured breathe-wrong nasal strips, we waited anxiously as Mark and Chip politely and quietly climbed into their racks, not wanting to disturb our "sleep". As soon as they got comfortable, we began to snore with intolerable volume in preplanned, pre-practiced harmonic rhythm. In snorted Jim, out snorted Roger, in snorted Roger, out snorted Jim. The breathe-wrong strips were apparently ineffective for me, and Jim seemed hopelessly controlled by sleep apnea. After listening to the unbearable noise for several minutes, Chip uttered to Mark, "Oh, no!" in slow and pained exasperation. Chip's comment and the manner in which it was so woefully expressed were far more than we could stand. We found it impossible to do anything but burst out laughing. Lights were turned on as I modeled the nasal strips that should have prevented the snoring fiasco. Our two exhausted brothers, Jim and I ended up cracking up together, praying and telling stories until five in the morning. We finally grabbed a few hours of sleep before a conference on Saturday morning. Our Ukrainian hosts did not sleep peacefully that night due to our unseemly decorum. They wondered about the entire ruckus but were too polite to ask us to quiet down.

The rest of the trip was awesome as our sleep-deprived team shared Jesus and our lives with hundreds of Ukrainians. Chip and Mark ended up meeting an interpreter who eventually helped Chip and his wife, Bethany, adopt a beautiful little Ukrainian girl, Kinza, a couple of years later. Chip, a devoted father of four, died suddenly and returned home to spend eternity with Jesus well ahead of our human schedule. A tragic accident at his workplace in December 2003 claimed the 38-year-old's life. I'll never forget the mission journey or Chip and look forward to our reunion in heaven. What foggy, yet beautiful memories of a great mission trip!

## MOTHER'S HELPER

A Ukrainian mother, Larissa, entered a clothing shop with her young daughter. The nine-year old girl's shoes were destined for the trash pile and no longer fit to wear. They were literally falling apart. We shared our reasons for sending the clothing and shoes. Larissa was amazed at how low the prices were, but yet the quality was so good. She was desperate to find a pair of good, used shoes for her daughter at an affordable price.

As she searched the shelves, her eyes were drawn to what looked like a brand new pair of dress shoes. And, they seemed to be appropriately sized. Sure enough, her daughter tried on the shoes and they fit perfectly, like Cinderella's slipper. The young girl jumped up and down with incredible excitement and jabbered away in Russian. It seemed like she was saying something like "Mommy, Mommy, look at these new shoes!" I thought back to my kids at home and how a new pair of shoes is so easy to obtain, and thus taken for granted by nearly all Americans. I'd never seen anyone excited over a pair of shoes. My eyes then met Larissa's eyes. I saw tears of joy streaming down her face, and I began to get choked up. Through the interpreter, she said, "Please give my thanks to whoever donated these shoes to help me take care of my daughter." She had paid the equivalent of 25 cents for that pair of shoes, but they were worth millions! WOW! The power of sending a pair of shoes in the name of Jesus! What a help to that young mother in her time of need!

## WARM WATERS

It's a refreshing privilege to work side-by-side with believers in other countries. You just do not often see lukewarm Christians overseas. Their level of devotion and commitment is commendable. Winter baptisms in Ukraine are acts of obedience that are especially inspiring. It's not uncommon for the men of the church to break the ice in order to provide access to the frigid waters. I guess you really cannot have a lukewarm faith and be willing to obey Christ in baptism in sub-forty degree waters.

In November 1999, Pastor Oleg Shishkin asked me to assist with a baptismal service. We gathered along with those to be baptized for a time of Bible study and prayer. After reviewing the purpose and significance of Christian baptism, Oleg talked about the harsh reality of the cold weather on that day. He instructed us that God's spiritual power would allow us to be warm even though it was a bitter cold and windy day. We were told not to waver in faith. God would keep us warm if we trusted Him and kept our eyes on Him. As we prayed, we trusted God to do what was not possible in the flesh. Six people were immersed that day. I remember sensing warmth as I entered the Dniepr River and felt comfortable physically during the time that I baptized half of the new believers that day. The cold did not hit me until we returned to the shore. It was amazing to experience the warm waters of Christian baptism thanks to God's supernatural intervention on that brisk November day. If God can enable Peter to walk on water, is He not able to make cold water feel warm? What is there that God cannot do?

## JUNIOR EVANGELIST

Kosova is one of the former Yugoslavian countries that began receiving shipments from MP in the third post-Christ millennium. Islam is the predominant religion there, and wide-scale, public evangelism is not permitted. As a result, it is a challenge to run a clothing outreach and let people explicitly know that the goods are provided in the name of Jesus. A wonderful mission in Kosova partners with us to receive and distribute clothing, shoes and other miscellaneous supplies in their country.

Our friend and field director in Kosova was led to take an entire shipment of humanitarian relief supplies, primarily clothing and shoes, to give to needy people in the mountain regions. All of the logistical details were resolved, and the precious cargo arrived in the rural village as thousands of excited Kosovars awaited receipt of the goods. Amidst the carnival-like atmosphere as volunteers began to distribute clothing and shoes, a young boy stood next to the director and tugged on his jacket to get his attention. He asked, "Sir, are these clothes and shoes from Allah?" The director replied, "No, these clothes and shoes are from believers in Jesus, the Jesus who loves you and died for you." The young boy unknowingly turned into an extreme evangelist for a couple of days. He ran around shouting: "These clothes are from Jesus, who loves you and died for you." "These clothes are from Jesus, who loves you and died for you." "These clothes are from Jesus, who loves you and died for you." And, so on and so on spread the Good News!

Little children are so useful to the work in God's Kingdom. We could have tried many different approaches to communicate our reasons for sharing tons of clothing and shoes with needy people in the mountains of Kosova. But, none could have so effectively told the story as a young Muslim boy that became a Junior Evangelist. He also effectively communicated a primary philosophy of MP: clothing is simply a tool to show people and tell them that Jesus loves and cares for them! God worked in a remarkable way to get that message across to thousands of Kosovars!

## BETHLEHEM TWO

In conjunction with Jesus Shine Ministries (JSM), we were introduced to the famed slums of urban India in December 2004. JSM exists to care for widows and orphans in and around the mega-city of Hyderabad. India is definitely a country of extremes and we were called to assist the extremely poor. Each day, we presented a Christmas Gospel message to mixed Hindu and Christian audiences ranging from 50 to 1,800 people. One day during our mission trip, a two-hour journey landed us in a remote village replete with dirt roads, block and thatch buildings and lots of cows and donkeys.

We gathered to worship outside of the tiny village church building, and hundreds of Indians crowded around to hear. While preaching a message about Jesus' birth to the crowd, I looked off in the distance and saw a young mother with a brand new baby, sitting under a thatch roof. Standing by her was a man with a staff that appeared to be her husband. Several other people and some animals joined the scene. My mind flashed back to what it may have looked like in a small burg in Israel on Jesus' birthday. I wanted to build a feeding trough and ask her if we could take a picture. The little town in India shall forever be remembered as Bethlehem Two.

## BICYCLE BRIGADE

Our wonderful transportation system makes it easy to collect and transport donated clothing and footwear from point to point within the United States. It is relatively easy to send containers from local packing and loading sites to a railroad terminal and on to the ocean port. Praise God, we can efficiently and swiftly send shipments of necessary items that become precious treasures in economically ravaged countries.

At the National Missionary Convention in Cincinnati during November 2003, a marvelous Christian brother, Paul Douglass, talked to us about sending a first shipment of clothing and footwear to help extremely poor people in Southern Sudan. War, religious persecution, tribal factions and extreme poverty make life arduous in that part of Africa. Since Sudan has no seaport, it would be tremendously difficult to get a container from Kenya to Sudan via Uganda on a 1,600-mile trek. The rugged dirt roads along much of the route make roads impassable for large trucks during rainy reasons. Plus, it would be extremely expensive to underwrite the project and probably impossible to find a trucker willing to traverse the dangerous route. However, I told Paul that God would honor his faith and provide both the funding and transportation to complete the project. Attendees at the conference and area churches would donate the clothing, and teens would sort, pack and load the container. All conferees were asked to bring offerings to defray expenses.

Through Paul's tireless efforts and God's provision, arrangements were finalized to actually send two 20-foot containers of clothing and footwear to the Aweil region of Southern Sudan. The containers had to be purchased since no international shipping company would allow their rented equipment to enter Sudan. That was actually a blessing, because the steel containers serve as valuable, secured warehouses and offices in impoverished rural areas in places like Sudan that have no storage options. Working in conjunction with Sudan African Mission, MP purchased the two containers for the project. The response in Peoria, Illinois, was outstanding, and a couple of twenty-foot-long containers were filled to the brim!

We delayed shipment about a month so that the final trucking leg of the delivery could occur during the dry season. The units arrived in Kenya in early February 2005, and reached their final destination in Sudan in late March. The difficult 6-week, 1,600-mile semi-truck journey involving two border crossings ended in success as the containers arrived in Aweil. Village pastors from 40 and more kilometers away completed multiple trips toting 80-pound sacks of clothing and shoes on the backs of their bicycles. They wrapped the clear plastic clothes bags in burlap or other materials so it would appear to passers-by that they were hauling grain or some other agricultural commodity. Thus, they were not easy prey for bandits, and all of the clothing and shoes ended up in the hands of our intended recipients by the end of summer, 2005.

Many Sudanese donned their first pair of shoes ever. Others were literally naked and received some nice clothing. *Ear-to-ear smiles marked the faces of the grateful recipients.* A successful bicycle brigade was the final step in delivering clothing and shoes to thousands of needy people in the name of Jesus, the very One who looks to see who is willing to clothe the naked!

## MOUNTAIN PHOTOGRAPHY

MASTER Provisions agreed to sponsor a clothes-packing project at Camp Allendale in Central Indiana in August 2005. During that day, we were privileged to meet Trevor and Valerie Colby, medical missionaries to Honduras. We also planned a field visit to Latin America since Colby Medical Missions was a new consignee for clothing containers.

**Ear-to-ear smiles marked the faces of the grateful recipients.**

The January 2006 trip to work with Trevor, Val and friends in Tegucigalpa, Honduras, led us to one of the poorest countries in the Western Hemisphere. Daily excursions into the beautiful Honduran mountains led us to impoverished communities. One day was certainly unforgettable. We locked in four-wheel drive when the roads became impassable for normal vehicles and continued to climb over 3,000 feet up a dangerous mountain dirt road. We could hardly imagine finding anyone in such a remote area.

Several of us bounced along as we stood in the back of the oversized pickup truck on top of bags of good used clothing. Along the way, we stopped a few times to pick up smiling Hondurans who were headed to the meeting place. Once we reached the summit, our load consisted of 2,400 pounds of clothing and 26 people. We pulled over at a mountain village and carried bags of clothing across a rickety footbridge suspended fifty feet above a river. Once across the river, we found a mission church and school and were shocked to greet a huge crowd of over 600 people. We learned that many had walked over two hours to obtain clothing and hear the good news about Jesus.

After teaching a Bible lesson to the children, we set up a makeshift photography studio in one of the modest classroom buildings. With the help of several interpreters, the Hondurans were instructed to gather in family groups and everyone would get a family photograph. Our daughter, Leah, willingly offered her photography services. I feebly attempted to serve as crowd controller and assistant for the "shoot". Our youngest daughter, Joy, and the other team members had glue, Popsicle sticks and markers to make colorful frames for the photos and write Scripture verses on them. *Very few of these people had ever seen their pictures before, and a family photo would become an instant keepsake.* The excitement and expectation in that room was incredible. The crowd anxiously pushed forward during the lengthy waiting period. We ended up with enough Polaroid film to produce exactly 120 treasures in a couple of hours. Not by our planning but by God's grace, we had just enough Polaroid packs to satisfy every waiting Honduran. How humbling it was to provide clothing and a photograph to hundreds of beautiful and thankful mountain people. Oh, the wonder of simple pleasures that become priceless treasures in daily mission work!

## MEANINGFUL MILK

Homogenized, pasteurized, whole milk, skim milk, 1%, 2%. No matter the fat content or treatment method used in processing, most children love to down a class of "moo" juice. Access to a glass of milk is taken for granted in some countries, but not so in Zimbabwe. Most children there are malnourished and not able to enjoy a cup of milk. Mr. Roy Wilson of Huntsville, Alabama, was burdened by this lack of life's most basic dairy product for Zimbabweans. So, he sent powdered milk on a shipment of clothing and medical supplies that he sponsored to be shipped to Zimbabwe.

We rejoiced as we saw pictures of long lines of children waiting for a drink of milk. Thousands of God's precious little ones were able to enjoy the tasty liquid. Southern Heights Christian

. . . . . . . . . . . . . . . . . . . . . . . . . . . . . . . . . . . . . .

**Very few of these people had ever seen their pictures before, and a family photo would become an instant keepsake.**

. . . . . . . . . . . . . . . . . . . . . . . . . . . . . . . . . . . . . .

Church in Lebanon, Missouri learned of this milk project and donated $1,000 toward the purchase of instant milk for the March 2006 shipment to Zimbabwe. Over 10,000 more Zimbabwe children waited at the milk pot to guzzle a delicious cup full of life's simple liquid pleasure. *Blessed are those who give a meaningful cup of water or milk in Jesus' name!*

### LEAH LEFT BEHIND

It was 5:00 a.m. Friday morning, January 20, 2006. A young lady stood at the airline check-in counter prepared to go on a mission trip she had eagerly anticipated for five months. The attendant said, "I'm sorry, you will not be able to go to Honduras. Your passport expires less than three months after your arrival, and they will not allow you to enter their country." What do you do? Leah Babik smiled and said, "If it's God's will, I'll see you in Honduras!" Her dad displayed obvious disappointment, but Leah's faith was remarkable for a sixteen-year old, or even for a sixty-year old gal.

We gave chauffeur and mom, Tanya, a quick call on the cell phone and asked her to take a U-turn back to the airport. In addition, we requested that Continental Airlines re-book Leah for Saturday's flights. The very last seat on both flights was assigned to Miss Babik. The airlines employee was incredibly helpful and even gave us her cell phone number so we could provide updated status on our attempts to obtain a passport in less than 24 hours.

> **Blessed are those who give a meaningful cup of water or milk in Jesus' name!**

Tanya returned home with instructions to check on same-day passport processing on the Internet. She printed forms and instructions, then made arrangements, in faith, to take a personal day off from work. Then, she whipped up lesson plans for a sub and returned home. Things looked bleak as Tanya opened the phone book about 8:00 a.m. With divine assistance, the book fell open to a page highlighting Senator Jim Bunning. She called the Senator's office and a most helpful lady cut through the governmental red tape and arranged a 2:30 p.m. appointment in Chicago for issuance of a new passport for Leah.

By 8:30 a.m., Leah and Tanya were bound for C-town after stopping to obtain passport photos. As they motored toward Chicago, Jim Smelser arranged for Leah and Tanya to meet a friend named Maureen Reiser (a veteran of MP mission travel) from Deer Creek Christian Church near Chicago at a train station. Maureen gave them a couple of sweaters since the girls hastily left home without jackets, and it was going to be a bitter winter day in the Windy City. Mrs. Reiser put them on a train destined for downtown Chicago. They arrived at the U.S. State Department 45 minutes late for their appointment and with less than an hour remaining in the workday. The government employee informed them it would take four to six hours to receive the passport, but, by God's grace and divine assistance, they walked out of the office, new passport in hand, before 4:00 p.m.

The Babik girls returned home about midnight and settled in for a less than adequate night's sleep. The weary travelers were back at the Continental check-in counter Saturday morning at 4:45 a.m. Leah joined the team in Honduras a day late and many hours of sleep short! Initially, it looked like Leah was left behind for good. However, God proved to be an awesome expediter for speedy passport renewal. He also honored Leah's faith!

*Part* 4
# A Challenge to Your Will

# CHAPTER 13

# How 'Bout You?

So much for learning about how God called a telephone man and then a team of people into full-time vocational Christian service. So much about the birth and growth of a mission and all of the wonderful things that God has done for me. What about you? Are you playing heavenly hide and seek with your Creator, who wants you to join Him in some aspect of Kingdom work? Are you engaged in a game of spiritual dodge ball? Is God trying to secure your talents for His glorious purposes and you keep running away from His call? That scenario sounds faithlessly familiar. ***It's time to get serious about knowing God's call and obeying it.***

Every committed Christian wants to please God. We do; we really do! If you could physically see a specific, handwritten set

**It's time to get serious about knowing God's call and obeying it.**

of instructions penned by the Creator's hand, you would follow them for sure, would you not? However, God's will is discerned spiritually, and I know of very few people who have heard audibly from the Lord. Fewer still have received written instructions from God, and none on record since before the time of Christ on earth. Consequently, we have to learn how to discern or hear from God spiritually in order to determine what He wants us to do. *Our Master has an absolute best plan laid out for each of our lives to maximize our usefulness to Him.* He patiently waits to see if we will discover that plan and then do it.

The most important eight-word sentence in the Bible finds God telling us like it is. I like His direct style. In fact, the only time He beat around the bush was when He spoke to Moses from the fiery shrub. God makes it abundantly clear that faith is an absolute requirement for pleasing Him: "Without faith it is impossible to please God!" (Hebrews 11:6, NIV) Faith in God is the starting and ending point for hearing, obeying and pleasing God. You cannot please God unless your decisions and your life are based in faith. The writer of Hebrews defines faith as being sure of what we hope for and certain of what we do not see. (Hebrews 11:1, NIV) Are you hoping for an avenue of service to God? Are you sure that is what you want to do? If so, put your total faith in God and stop looking back. Have faith that God will:

- do more than you can see
- do more than you ask or imagine
- do what is best

**Our Master has an absolute best plan laid out for each of our lives to maximize our usefulness to Him.**

- give you everything that you need for life and godliness
- not give you more than you can handle
- will absolutely not ask you to do anything that would harm you or bring you despair.

We know that all people who ready themselves for noble purposes will be useful to God and prepared to do any good work (2 Timothy 2:21). A life marked by pursuit of a relationship with the Lord and a desire to serve Him is a life that is ready to follow God's call. Are you regularly asking God to reveal to you what He wants you to do?

Determining what you are hearing and who is calling is perhaps our biggest challenge and difficulty. We must distinguish between our personal desires, Satan's deceptive lures and God's call. Our ultimate goal is for our desires to match God's call. Satan will always be looming in his role as deceiver to tempt and trick you. Be sure, he will always cast doubt on your mind.

Timing is an important factor in determining the source of a call on your life. Following God's call will always seem inconvenient in the fleshly realm. To your physical senses, it will never seem like the right time to take a leap of faith and obedience. God will always patiently wait for you to respond, whereas Satan and self demand hasty decisions that must be made without time for prayer and meditation. If you are sensing time urgency in

**When God calls, you will sense peace, calm and a lack of hurriedness, even though you will simultaneously feel challenged in your faith and almost overwhelmed in the flesh. Trust and obey.**

responding to a call, then commit to pray and wait. *When God calls, you will sense peace, calm and a lack of hurriedness, even though you will simultaneously feel challenged in your faith and almost overwhelmed in the flesh.* Trust and obey.

Excuses will surface regularly when God makes a call on your life. Satan will drum up the excuses while God patiently awaits your decision. May I suggest some common excuses that will enter your thought life? Perhaps an excuse checklist would help you. Please place the date on the line to the right of the excuse that represents the day you first conceived it.

- Now is just not the right time in my life! _____
- How will others feel about this decision? _____
- I'm not fully prepared for this assignment! _____
- I would have to move to do this. _____
- I would really miss my family and friends. _____
- Perhaps I should wait until after I retire. _____
- How will I take care of "my" expenses? _____
- Other people can do this better than I can. _____
- My kids aren't grown up yet. _____
- What if things don't work out as planned? _____
- How will we pay for the kids to attend college? _____
- I don't know the language over there. _____
- My salary and benefits will be cut severely. _____
- Will people accept me in this role? _____
- What if people know about my past mistakes? _____
- Does this really need to be done? _____
- I don't have time in my schedule to do this. _____
- There will be some things I miss out on. _____

The excuses come from one of the two "S" sources, Self or Satan. Be sure such doubts and excuses will arise. Satan is the master of doubts, fears and illusions, and he certainly does not want you to step out in faith and trust God. Satan will bombard you with thoughts designed to distract, discourage or delay your decision. Mark it down! *You will get distracted, delayed and discouraged by the deceiver when God calls you to His service!*

Jesus showed us what to do when Satan sends worthless thoughts your way. Use Scripture to counteract him. Use the name of Jesus to fight our spiritual foe. Satan mocks and laughs at the name of Roger Babik, but he runs at the mention of Jesus Christ. Let your enemy know that you are God's child and you will obey His call, no matter the cost, when that is what you truly believe. Tell Satan: "In the name of Jesus, get behind me because you do not have in mind the things of God!" "Here am I, send me!" is a powerful response, first offered by Isaiah, that Satan despises.

*Your gifts, talents and abilities form an important basis for God's call on your life.* God wants to give you all good things to enjoy, and He wants you to do things that are inherently enjoyable for you. He designed you and will give you things to do for Him that utilize the talents and gifts that He gave you at conception and that have been developed over the years. If God is calling you to some type of service, the duty will match your abilities and interests. And, that service makes you happy, filled with joy and comes naturally. It will not be a struggle to complete the work God gives you to do. You would do that task for God even if there were never any pay or benefits in this life.

**You will get distracted, delayed and discouraged by the deceiver when God calls you to His service!**

God will often use life experiences that you have had prior to connecting with Him in full-time Christian vocational service. For me, God knew that MASTER Provisions would require a business mind and administrative gifts. One of my primary task-oriented gifts is administration. I totally enjoy managing a job down to the tiny details and following through to successful completion. I'm a "make a list, check it twice" type of person. It may sound bizarre to many people, but that activity is fun for me. Consequently, God gave me five years of experience as a market administrator to hone those skills in the business world.

Two of my relational gifts are speaking and encouragement. Success in mission ministry involves working with and speaking to many different audiences. I love to speak to groups, no matter how large, and even get energized thinking about an upcoming opportunity to talk to people. Volunteers need a regular dose of sincere encouragement to handle the mundane and sometimes strenuous jobs associated with packing and loading large quantities of clothing and shoes. Encouraging words flow naturally from my lips like water over Niagara Falls. I love to offer encouragement to others, and such words abound as I spur others on to love and good deeds. To help put my gifts of speaking and encouragement into practice, God gave me six years of experience in managing and motivating people in the business world. In addition, the Lord provided seven years of practice in selling products and services that required daily speaking and presentations for success. The past experience in the business

**Your gifts, talents and abilities form an important basis for God's call on your life.**

world superbly prepared me to lead a unique and growing mission ministry!

I suggest an exercise that you should perform if you are wondering whether God is calling you to some new venture for Him. Write down your gifts and talents. Then, see if the calling and challenge presented to you will utilize those abilities. If there is a match and you get excited thinking about doing that task every day for God, He could well be calling you to His service. God will not call you to a task and then make it drudgery for you. The very thought of performing that service or ministry full-time will fill you with excitement and eager anticipation.

True blessings related to your obedience to God's call will not flow into your life until you make a firm commitment to obey God. Therefore, you should not expect to see a windfall of new heavenly blessings as you contemplate a call to full-time service. In fact, God may allow a time of testing that includes some relative hardships as you weigh the decision. In addition, your eternal enemy is acting within his realm of evil to try to prevent you from fully obeying God. *But, oh, the cascade from God's fountain of blessings that is possible once your vocational choice aligns with His will.*

While evaluating God's call on your life, plan to devote yourself to a time of prayer and fasting in order to sharpen your spiritual discernment and to obtain answers from God. A huge spiritual battle will take place as unseen wars are waged to influence your decision and allegiance. The oft-neglected discipline of fast-

**But, oh, the cascade from God's fountain of blessings that is possible once your vocational choice aligns with His will.**

ing will aid you in this conflict. *It is amazing what fasting will do for your ability to connect with God and his infallible wisdom.* Fasting takes your focus off of your physical needs and enables you to hear clearly from God through His Spirit and His Word. Don't cut short your time of fasting. Enter this period of fasting with a specific purpose to get specific answers to your questions. Continue to fast until you receive the answers for the questions that you have asked of God. Fasting will also give you the extra strength that you need to fight the spiritual battle that will take place as you contemplate taking a big step of faith vocationally.

During the contemplation period, you need to summon together a band of prayer partners. Ask this trusted group of confidantes to pray daily for you to hear spiritually from God so that your will can match His will. They should pray that God would confirm this calling to you in different ways. Also, ask them to have God tell them what you are supposed to be doing. As they come to prayerfully drawn conclusions, everyone on the prayer team will eventually be led to the same decision. For God is a God of unity and consistency, and He will not tell opposing things to different people.

God continues to reconfirm or clarify His call in whatever manner He needs to do to fully get your attention. God uses circumstances and other people as the two most common methods to reconfirm His call on your life. Things will happen during your decision period to help you understand God's will. God's call is a work, or process, and not a single event. He is already at work on

**God simply wants your will to yield to His perfect and sovereign plans for your life!**

you, inside of you and around you. However, He will not barge His way through your human will. ***God simply wants your will to yield to His perfect and sovereign plans for your life!***

Think about Saul-Paul, the greatest evangelist of natural human conception who ever walked the planet. He lived over half his years in unknowing rebellion to God, but God was at work around him. As he consented to the stoning of Stephen and others, God was showing Saul the courage and faith it took to be a true follower of Christ. It required a very unusual circumstance, a heavenly light show, to literally blind Saul into submission. After temporarily losing physical eyesight, he experienced new birth and learned the true Gospel. Paul was then unleashed on the world, ready to follow God's call. God prepared him for His service through various experiences and events. The rest of Paul's life was lived in unashamed usefulness to the glory of God!

So, how 'bout you? What are you waiting for? Say "yes" to your Heavenly Father, Creator and Provider if He is calling you into full-time service. From the moment that you fully obey God's call, you will experience a spiritual euphoria unlike nothing else (except perhaps the day that Jesus Christ became your Lord and Savior). You will never look back with regrets to your days of corporate captivity or other employment. In fact, you may have to pinch yourself every once in a while to remind yourself that your newfound calling is for real. It just doesn't seem like work when you enjoy what you are doing so much. If God called you to do it, be sure that you will experience a contentment and satisfaction with your work that you never thought possible. Trust God! Follow His call now, even if it seems contrary to your will or public opinion! Let the eternal benefits begin!

# QUICK ORDER FORM

**Fax orders:** 859-525-6897.  Please send this form.

**Telephone orders:**  Call 859-816-6087.  Please have your credit card ready.  MasterCard and Visa only.

**Email orders:** roger@masterprovisions.org

**Postal orders:**  MASTER Provisions, Roger Babik, 12236 Hutton Drive, Walton, KY  41094.  Please send this form.

**Please:** ___  send information about MASTER Provisions
           ___  contact me regarding Speaking Engagements
           ___  send information on MASTER Care Orphan Ministry
           ___  add me to the MASTER Provisions mailing list
           ___  send updates about MASTER Provisions via Email

Name _____

Address _____

City _____ State _____ Zip _____

Phone (with area code) _____

Email address _____

**Quantity of Books Ordered:** _____

**Cost/Payment:**  Please submit $12.95 per book, which includes shipping costs to domestic locations in the United States.  Make checks payable to MASTER Provisions.  Visa and MasterCard accepted:

Card Number: _____

Expiration Date:  Month _____  Year_____

**International:**  Please send $12.95 per book plus add $10.00 per book shipping for the first book and $6.00 per book for each additional book ordered.

# QUICK ORDER FORM

**Fax orders:** 859-525-6897. Please send this form.

**Telephone orders:** Call 859-816-6087. Please have your credit card ready. MasterCard and Visa only.

**Email orders:** roger@masterprovisions.org

**Postal orders:** MASTER Provisions, Roger Babik, 12236 Hutton Drive, Walton, KY 41094. Please send this form.

**Please:** ___ send information about MASTER Provisions
___ contact me regarding Speaking Engagements
___ send information on MASTER Care Orphan Ministry
___ add me to the MASTER Provisions mailing list
___ send updates about MASTER Provisions via Email

Name _____

Address _____

City _____ State _____ Zip _____

Phone (with area code) _____

Email address _____

**Quantity of Books Ordered:** _____

**Cost/Payment:** Please submit $12.95 per book, which includes shipping costs to domestic locations in the United States. Make checks payable to MASTER Provisions. Visa and MasterCard accepted:

Card Number: _____

Expiration Date: Month _____ Year_____
**International:** Please send $12.95 per book plus add $10.00 per book shipping for the first book and $6.00 per book for each additional book ordered.